⊗»»»— THE MOUNTAINS ARE CALLING —«««⊗

MOUNT SHUKSAN, WASHINGTON

THE MOUNTAINS ARE CALLING

YEAR-ROUND ADVENTURES in the OLYMPICS and WEST CASCADES

NANCY BLAKEY

SASQUATCH BOOKS
SEATTLE

To the volunteers who dig, lift, build, clear, and groom our trails. May the Forest be with you.

—

Printed in South Korea

SASQUATCH BOOKS with colophon is a registered trademark of Penguin Random House LLC

26 25 24 23 22   9 8 7 6 5 4 3 2 1

Illustrations: Chandler O'Leary
Photography: Nick Hall
Editor: Hannah Elnan
Production editors: Jill Saginario, Rachelle Longé McGhee
Designer: Tony Ong

Photo on page 152 by Joel Gaff on Unsplash
Photo on page 158 by Sean Estergaard on Unsplash

Library of Congress Cataloging-in-Publication Data
Names: Blakey, Nancy, author.
Title: The mountains are calling : year-round adventures in the Olympics
   and West Cascades / Nancy Blakey.
Description: Seattle, WA : Sasquatch Books, 2022. | Includes bibliographical
   references and index.
Identifiers: LCCN 2021015404 (print) | LCCN 2021015405 (ebook) | ISBN
   9781632173218 (paperback) | ISBN 9781632173225 (ebook)
Subjects: LCSH: Outdoor recreation--Washington (State)--Olympic
   Mountains--Guidebooks. | Outdoor recreation--Cascade Range--Guidebooks.
   | Olympic Mountains (Wash.)--Guidebooks. | Cascade Range--Guidebooks.
Classification: LCC GV191.42.W2 B58 2022 (print) | LCC GV191.42.W2 (ebook)
   | DDC 917.97/9404--dc23
LC record available at https://lccn.loc.gov/2021015404
LC ebook record available at https://lccn.loc.gov/2021015405

ISBN: 978-1-63217-321-8

Sasquatch Books
1904 Third Avenue, Suite 710
Seattle, WA 98101

SasquatchBooks.com

Cover photo: Mount Baker Nooksack River

Contents

TANK LAKE, ALPINE LAKES WILDERNESS AREA

The mountains are calling
and I must go . . .

—JOHN MUIR

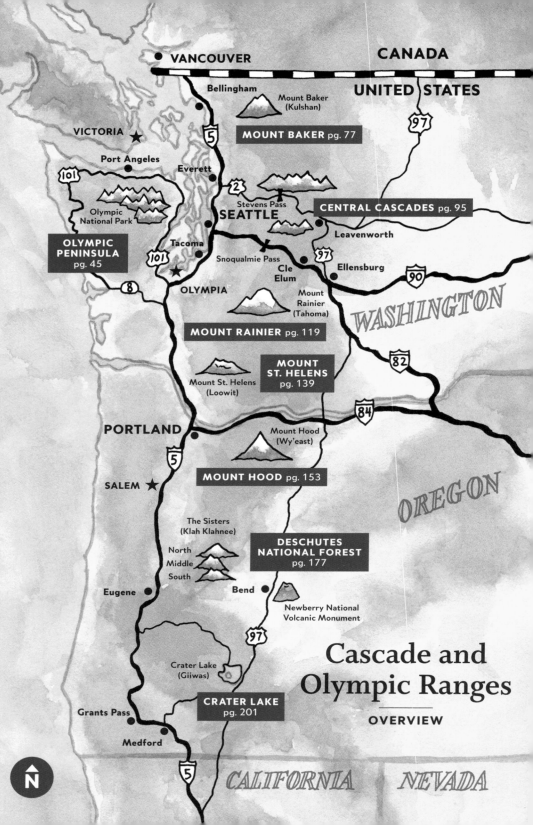

VANCOUVER

CANADA

UNITED STATES

Bellingham

Mount Baker
(Kulshan)

97

MOUNT BAKER pg. 77

VICTORIA ★

Port Angeles

Everett

101

2

Stevens Pass

CENTRAL CASCADES pg. 95

Leavenworth

5

Olympic
National Park

SEATTLE

**OLYMPIC
PENINSULA**
pg. 45

101

Tacoma

Snoqualmie Pass

Cle
Elum

97

Ellensburg

90

8

OLYMPIA

WASHINGTON

Mount
Rainier
(Tahoma)

MOUNT RAINIER pg. 119

82

**MOUNT
ST. HELENS**
pg. 139

Mount St. Helens
(Loowit)

84

PORTLAND

Mount Hood
(Wy'east)

5

MOUNT HOOD pg. 153

SALEM ★

OREGON

The Sisters
(Klah Klahnee)

North

Middle

South

**DESCHUTES
NATIONAL FOREST**
pg. 177

Eugene

Bend

97

Newberry National
Volcanic Monument

Crater Lake
(Giiwas)

Cascade and
Olympic Ranges

OVERVIEW

CRATER LAKE
pg. 201

Grants Pass

Medford

5

N

CALIFORNIA

NEVADA

Introduction

The mountains are calling. Did you answer with a maybe or a no, waiting for better weather, for more time, or for the kids to grow up? Waiting for the right gear, a companion, or to get more fit? Not to worry. This is your book of yes, of now—whatever shape you're in or whatever the weather. Bring the baby, pack a picnic, put on your walking shoes, and head out the door. You don't need to be über fit, own high-tech equipment, or enjoy roughing it. You need only the hunger for more than screen time and a willingness to get out of your comfort zone and explore with family and friends, or perhaps alone. For some that may mean your first car-camping trip, for others a solo wilderness hike. No matter your threshold for adventure, it all takes risk, and it all brings reward. The glorious Pacific Northwest is full of mountains and lakes and rivers—some right outside the back door or a short drive away—and now is the time to enjoy them.

This book is your invitation to hike woodlands or plan an epic multiday trek, to enjoy lodges and campgrounds, to see waterfalls and wildflowers, to soak in hot springs. The Pacific Northwest is studded with mountain ranges that would take volumes to cover in depth. Instead, this book offers a taste of the Coast Range and the western part of the Washington and Oregon Cascades for people starting to hear and heed the call of the mountains but not sure where to begin. The activities emphasize car camping and using the campground as a launchpad for multiday activities. The parks and recreation areas covered were chosen for their proximity to the urban centers of Seattle and Portland for easy weekends away, for the availability of easy to moderate hikes, and for the Scenic Byways taken to reach them. I also chose them out of my own love of hidden gems. This is a book of ideas to spark your Pacific Northwest mountain adventures.

NORTH SISTER, OREGON

PART I

MOUNTAIN BASICS

MOUNT BAKER, WASHINGTON

How to Use This Book

Part 1 contains all the know-before-you-go information. Following this are three other parts about where to go and what to do when you get there: the Coast Range, which contains the Olympic Peninsula; the Washington Cascades; and the Oregon Cascades. Within the Cascades sections, there are seven chapters focusing on individual mountain regions—all concentrate largely on the west side, and they are organized from north to south. Each mountain region chapter has a selection of places to stay, including campgrounds, cabins, and lodges to use as a base camp for your outdoor adventures. Then you'll find activities divided into Season of Green and Season of Snow, offering a wide variety of experiences relevant to the time of year. The green sections generally cover spring, summer, and autumn months, and focus on hiking and backpacking. The snow sections cover winter and snow sports, but there is considerable overlap between the seasons, particularly when a cold spring can hold snow on the flanks of mountains deep into summer or when a warmer winter opens trails in February. Check the trail conditions before you go in Washington (*wta .org*) and in Oregon (*alltrails.com* or *oregonhikers.org*) for the latest beta reports from others who have hiked your chosen trail.

Throughout the book, individual mountains or ranges are sometimes called by their Native American name. Indigenous peoples were the original inhabitants of all mountain regions in the Pacific Northwest, and they observed, named, and honored the mountains and their geological features long before non-Natives arrived. A multitude of different tribes flourished in the areas covered in this guide, using many different names for their mountains; I chose the most commonly known Native name to include for each. As we enjoy all the Pacific Northwest has to offer, let's remember and acknowledge the Native peoples who walked here before, and those who are here still.

The featured hikes and activities are only a taste of the great feast each mountain range offers and focus on easy and moderate routes. Each hike entry in the book includes the following:

Name of hike

Pass needed at the trailhead

Icons for quick reference (check out the hike index that lists all day hikes by length and icon on page 219)

☺ **BEGINNER AND FAMILY FRIENDLY:** Easy hikes with points of interest for little hikers and novices. Short (generally under 3 miles) and take 1 to 3 hours to complete depending on kid speed.

♨ **NEAR A CAMPGROUND:** A short walk or drive from a campground, making it easy to use a campsite as a base.

✿ **WILDFLOWERS:** Most mountain hikes have wildflowers, but this designation indicates exceptional sweeps of flowers in season, generally early May through August.

🌿 **BERRY PICKING:** Autumn hikes with easy access to blueberries and huckleberries from the trail.

🐦 **BIRD-WATCHING:** Hikes with a broader habitat and a wider variety of birds than commonly found on other trails.

🐾 **DOGS ALLOWED:** Most state parks and national forests have dog-friendly hikes. Dogs must be kept on a leash less than 8 feet long.

★ **WOW FACTOR:** May have a big elevation gain and take work to complete, but the views or landscape are out of this world.

〰 **WATERFALL:** Hikes that feature a great number of waterfalls or extraordinary waterfalls.

♿ **ACCESSIBLE:** Generally this means paved trails that are wheelchair and stroller friendly. If unpaved, suitable for all-terrain wheelchairs and jogging strollers. Specific conditions noted in hike description.

Level of difficulty

- EASY: Mostly flat, little elevation gain, and a well-defined trail with even footing. Usually under 3 miles. Suitable for children and beginner hikers.
- MODERATE: Some elevation gain (generally up to 2,000 feet) with the possibility of short steep sections and switchbacks. Trails may be rougher and narrower than easy hikes, with some roots and rocks to navigate and possible creek crossings. Usually 5 to 10 miles in length. Suitable for anyone who is reasonably active.
- DIFFICULT: Significant elevation gain (more than 2,000 feet) with rugged trails. May need a degree of skill and strong knees. Can be short (less than 5 miles) but tend to be longer than moderate hikes and may take all day to complete. Climbs can be long, and footing irregular or uneven. Suitable for strong hikers who are fitter than average.
- NOTE: Some hikes are rated *moderate to difficult* if the trail is moderate in sections and difficult in others. Use common sense when deciding which hike is for you.

Mileage and whether it's a loop or out-and-back

Elevation gain or loss

Approximate hike time (if your pace averages 2 miles per hour)

Short description of the hike

- Each description ends with a homepage URL for the regional website that provides details about the hike and directions to the trailhead; simply type the hike name into the search bar of the provided web address. Many of the sites also offer the latest beta information on trail conditions by fellow hikers. Note that it's important to visit the local ranger station or visitor center for permits, maps, and the weather forecast before setting out.

If you want to explore more, check out the bibliography for excellent guides that will lead you farther and deeper into the mountains with detailed information. Remember, on all your outdoor adventures, leave no trace! That means packing out toilet paper, cigarette butts, used chewing gum, dog poop, and all fruit peels, including banana and citrus—they do not decompose well and are not part of the natural environment in the Pacific Northwest.

Read on! The adventure begins.

SUBALPINE WILDFLOWERS

OREGON SUNSHINE: Named for its bright, sunny head, Oregon sunshine is a hardy and early bloomer, generally blooming from May through August along bluffs, rocky slopes, and dry open habitats.

PAINTBRUSH: Easy to identify with its vivid scarlet bracts, it's found throughout the Pacific Northwest in open forests, grasslands, hillsides, and meadows. Paintbrush blooms late June through August.

AVALANCHE LILY: A source of food for indigenous Northwest tribes, the graceful avalanche lily blossoms in alpine meadows and moist open areas, often near melting snow, from June through August.

SPREADING PHLOX: The low-growing lavish mats of lavender flowers are found in open rocky slopes and scree. They are long bloomers from mid-spring through August.

FANLEAF CINQUEFOIL: This early summer bloomer is found in higher elevation subalpine areas in moist meadows and scree slopes.

BROADLEAF LUPINE: A tall and graceful wildflower found in moist habitats and open meadows, the lupine begins to bloom in the late spring and early summer months.

BEAR GRASS: Showy flowers on tall stems emerge from a clump of grasslike leaves. Bears love to eat the young fleshy stems, giving this wildflower its name. Bear grass can be found in the forest understory of the Cascade Mountains, as well as in open meadows, and can begin blooming in late May through August at higher elevations.

ELEPHANT'S HEAD: The tightly packed clusters of flowers fill a stem that grows up to 16 inches tall and bear a striking resemblance to an elephant's head. The plant is found in mid- to high-elevation meadows late June through August.

WHY LEAVE NO TRACE?

Good outdoor recreationists know to leave no trace. It takes years, sometimes centuries, for certain materials to decompose.

- **DOG POOP:** Depending on weather conditions and elevation, 9 weeks to 12 months
- **TOILET PAPER:** If buried 6 inches deep in damp soil conditions, just 6 weeks; if disposed of improperly (under a rock, for example, or left on the ground), 1 to 2 years
- **CIGARETTE BUTTS:** Depending on conditions, 18 months to 10 years
- **FRUIT PEELS:** 6 months (oranges); 2 years or more (bananas)
- **SUNFLOWER AND PISTACHIO SHELLS:** 3 years in damp conditions; decades in dry conditions
- **DOG-WASTE BAG:** 10 to 20 years
- **WET WIPE:** 100 years (because of the plastic material)
- **PLASTIC BOTTLE:** 450 years
- **ENERGY BAR WRAPPER:** Never—foil doesn't decompose
- **CHEWING GUM:** Never—it's made from synthetic rubber that doesn't decompose

MOUNT ST. HELENS, WASHINGTON

In the Mountains 101

Confused about the different types of public lands? Know which recreation pass you'll need at the trailhead? Worried about bears? Not sure what to bring in your day pack? Here's the basic information you need to help you become a more skilled adventurer.

Types of Public Lands

Public lands belong to all of us and there are different types, each with their own rules. For example, dogs are not allowed in national parks, but they are allowed in national forests. Here are the types of public lands you'll encounter in your Pacific Northwest mountain explorations:

- NATIONAL PARKS: Lands protected and designated by Congress for their inherent scenic, inspirational, and cultural assets.
- NATIONAL FORESTS: Usually designated near national parks; managed for multiple uses, with lumber, grazing, and mineral extraction allowed in addition to recreation.
- NATIONAL MONUMENTS: Areas permanently protected and designated by the President for their unique historical, cultural, or scientific attributes. Mount St. Helens is one example.
- WILDERNESS AREAS: These federally managed lands are protected by Congress from development of any kind. There are many rules and regulations in these pristine wildernesses, such as traveling only on foot and hiking in groups of less than 10 people. Can be within national parks, national forests, public lands, or refuges. Visit the US Forest Service website for a complete list of rules.
- NATIONAL RECREATION AREAS: Designated near a large reservoir for visitors to enjoy water-based activities such as swimming, boating, fishing, and paddle sports.
- WILD AND SCENIC RIVERS: This designation preserves and enhances free-flowing rivers or river segments to keep the surrounding land in its natural condition. The river must possess at least one "outstandingly remarkable value." Less than a quarter of 1 percent of US rivers are protected under the National Wild and Scenic Rivers System, even

though tens of thousands of river miles are eligible. Bottom line: The designation takes an act of Congress.

- STATE PARKS: Typically smaller than national parks and managed at the state level.

What You Will Need: Recreation Passes

You'll need a permit to display in your car for hikes at most developed trailheads. Funding for national forests and parks has been in decline over the years despite the increase in use, and the permits play a critical role in helping to keep the wilderness wild and the trails maintained. Buy annual passes and keep them in your glove box; you'll save time on your hiking day and be ready to hit the trails at a moment's notice.

WASHINGTON

Although the various agencies running the trailheads offer different day passes, two annual passes will cover you in the state of Washington:

- America the Beautiful Pass (*store.usgs.gov*): The best deal around. It provides entrance to all national parks, national forests, and federal sites that charge a fee, such as Bureau of Land Management areas.
- Washington Discover Pass (*discoverpass.wa.gov*): This pass covers all Washington state parks and Washington State Department of Natural Resources lands. Buy one when you renew your car tabs each year.

Without an America the Beautiful Pass, you'll need a Northwest Forest Pass (*store.usgs.gov*) for all national forest trailheads (federal land).

Washington Sno-Park permits allow you to park in the winter at plowed lots that access groomed and backcountry trails. The permits provide funding to groom trails, remove snow from parking lots, and provide other winter services. They can be purchased online from November 1 to April 30. *epermits.parks.wa.gov*

Backcountry or wilderness permits are required for all overnight backcountry camping in all national parks or quota areas like the Enchantments in the Washington Cascades. Backcountry permits regulate the number of hikers to protect fragile environments and offer a less congested experience. Information on backcountry permits and advance lottery reservation windows is available at the individual parks' visitor centers. If the reservation window is closed, national parks hold a certain number of daily first-come, first-served permits. Get to the visitor center early in the morning of hike day to increase your odds of securing one.

OREGON

You'll need only the America the Beautiful Pass for the featured places in this book, with the exception of a Sno-Park permit in winter at Sno-Parks. Alternately, a Northwest Forest Pass covers the activities only in national forests. If you don't want to buy annual passes, buy a daily permit at the trailhead.

Backcountry or wilderness permits are required for overnights in all national parks.

In the winter months, Oregon's Sno-Parks require a valid Sno-Park permit between November 1 and April 30. Permits are sold at all Driver and Motor Vehicle Services offices or at the vendors listed at *oregon.gov /odot/dmv.*

Car Camping Tips and Tricks

- Arrive in camp with a full tank of gas. Gas stations can be few and far between in the mountains.
- Store food in the car at night to deter bears and critters.
- Slip a headlamp around a gallon jug of water, with the lens side facing the plastic, to illuminate your tent with ambient light.
- Freeze water in plastic jugs and bottles and use them in the cooler instead of loose ice.
- Make fire starters by rubbing petroleum jelly onto cotton balls. Store in a ziplock bag.
- Bring a Frisbee and after playing, clean it and use as a plate or cutting board. It can also be a shovel in emergencies.
- Before you leave, crack any eggs you'll need into a reusable water bottle and store in your cooler.
- Place spices in a weekly plastic vitamin or medicine container and relabel the top.
- Make a handwashing station by placing a bar of soap in a nylon stocking; tie one end of the nylon around the handle of a plastic gallon jug filled with water.
- Use cheap solar-powered lights around your campsite to light the way back to the tent.

Hiking Rules of the Trail

- There's a hierarchy on the trail: horses have priority, then hikers, then mountain bikers, who must yield to both horses and hikers. When you are passed by a horse, stand on the downhill side when possible; horses tend to bolt uphill when spooked.
- Give way to the uphill hiker.
- Stay on the trail! Erosion is easy to start and hard to stop.
- Keep to the right and pass on the left. When approaching another hiker from behind, call out a friendly "hello" or "on your left."
- When taking a break, move carefully off the trail so others can pass easily.
- Leave no trace! If you packed it in, pack it out, including banana peels, used gum, and toilet paper.
- If hiking in a group, don't crowd out the trail—leave enough space for those behind you to pass.
- Don't feed the wildlife! It interferes with their natural foraging habits and makes them pests.
- Limit device use on the trail. There's plenty of time for that at home.

THE CHANGING FACE OF OUTDOOR RECREATIONISTS

Enjoying nature under a wide sky is a universal pleasure. The forests and mountains accept all, but access to the wilderness and public lands hasn't always been easy for people of color. There's a long history of systemic racism, economic barriers, and the feeling of "otherness" out on the trail, but that's changing with the increasing number of people across demographic and social spectrums spending more time outdoors. Encouraging outdoor recreation for all people is important, and Latinx writer David Robles offers five ways to build a more inclusive hiking community in an excellent and relevant essay. *melaninbasecamp.com/robles-bio*

Multiday-Hike Gear List

Keep your pack trim for the trail. Balance your choices with the essentials and the extras you are willing to carry.

THE 10 ESSENTIALS
Bring on any hike, regardless of length.

1   Navigation: maps, compass, and/or GPS
2   Headlamp with extra batteries
3   First aid kit
4   Pocketknife
5   Sunscreen
6   Waterproof matches or lighter
7   Shelter (such as a lightweight emergency blanket)
8   Extra food
9   Extra water
10 Extra layers of clothing

OTHER ESSENTIAL GEAR

- Tent
- Sleeping bag and pad
- Water filter or purifying tablets
- Food
- Waterproof matches or lighter

IMPORTANT GEAR

- Stove and fuel
- Cooking and eating utensils, mug, and bowl
- Water bottles
- Waterproof rain gear
- Pack cover
- Insect repellent
- Bandana
- Safety whistle to use if lost, to send an alarm, or to warn bears of your presence while hiking
- Lightweight trowel to dig holes for human waste

HOW TO PACK A BACKPACK

NAVIGATION

HEAD LAMP

FIRST AID KIT

POCKET KNIFE

SUNSCREEN

FIRE STARTER

EMERGENCY SHELTER

EXTRA FOOD AND WATER

EXTRA LAYERS OF CLOTHING

CAMERA

THE 10 ESSENTIALS

CLOTHING

FOOD

TENT POLES

COOKING GEAR

TENT

SLEEPING BAG

BED ROLL

- 30 feet of parachute cord to hang food from a tree, make a clothesline, etc.
- Several layers of duct tape wound around a water bottle
- Blister kit (see Blisters 101, page 31)
- Toilet paper and a ziplock bag to pack it out
- Trekking poles and snow and ice footwear traction that fits over your boots for grip at higher elevations with slow snowmelt
- Personal toiletries and medicines

CLOTHING

- Down jacket
- Quick-dry hiking pants with zip-off legs to make shorts
- Synthetic or wool long-sleeved top and t-shirt for day use
- Synthetic or wool long johns to sleep in
- Hat and gloves
- Midweight synthetic fleece
- Extra wool or synthetic socks (wet feet are prone to blisters)
- Sandals to use as camp shoes and for river crossings

OPTIONAL BUT NICE TO HAVE

- Coffee maker
- Cleanup kit: small piece of sponge with a scrubber backing, biodegradable soap
- Small piece of lightweight plastic to use as a cutting board
- Stuff sacks to keep backpack organized
- Extra ziplock bags
- Pack towel
- Camp chair
- Sketchbook and pens
- Small binoculars
- Reading material

Make It Easy on Yourself: Lightweight Backpacking

Many beginner backpackers carry too much weight in their packs. A lighter backpack keeps you nimble on your feet, puts less stress on creaky knees, reduces fatigue, and decreases the chance of injury. Get organized. List all the gear and jot down its weight. Lay everything out to see what you'll be carrying. Aim for 20 to 30 pounds on your back, but it's not necessary to spend an exorbitant amount of money to have all the ultralight gear. Use your hiking budget to go lightweight on the four heaviest items (besides food and water): tent, sleeping bag, sleeping pad, and backpack. You can shave off several pounds by using a smaller backpack that will force you to take less.

- Cut the things you don't need, but find the sweet spot between bringing both essential items and the gear you want in order to be comfortable in camp.
- Hike with a partner to distribute the weight. Divide tent poles and tent, fuel and stove, food and cooking utensils.
- Repackage food and toiletries into ziplock bags.
- Use dehydrated food; avoid too many fresh fruits and vegetables.
- Water is heavy! Carry 1 liter, and plan on filtering water at creeks and lakes along the way. Consider buying a mini filter/purifier, and use a collapsible water bottle to save weight.
- Bring only the clothes you need. If you are out for a few days, re-wear the same clothes. To keep your sleeping bag clean, sleep in synthetic or wool long johns. Bring a clean pair of socks for each day on shorter hikes (wet feet invite blisters).
- Pare down the first aid kit to blister bandages, regular bandages, antibiotic ointment packets, pain-relief pills, and a few alcohol wipes.

Backpacking Bonus Tricks

These items take up little room and can save the day:

- Line your pack with a plastic compactor bag, which is sturdier than a regular garbage bag. Pack your gear inside to keep everything dry even in the heaviest downpours.
- Bring trick birthday candles for a fire starter, the kind that restart over and over.

ODE TO SOLO HIKING

Are you longing to head to the mountains but no one can join you? Go anyway. Solo hiking is a walking meditation without anyone to distract you from your own musings. You can move at your own pace, stop when you want, pick berries, take photos, sketch, problem solve. There is no one to wait for. Self-confidence blooms. Start with a day hike. You have nothing to lose, and everything to gain.

CRATER LAKE, OREGON

- Dry wet shoes overnight by stuffing them with dry dirty clothes or wads of newspaper. Newspaper is another multiuse item for reading material as well as a fire starter.
- Stow several extra-high-calorie bars in case you're out on the trail longer than expected.
- Pack a space blanket to retain body warmth in a storm or unexpected cold temperatures.

COMMON HIKING AND CAMPING TERMS

BACKCOUNTRY: Remote areas of public lands or national parks that are accessible by trails and not by roads

BACKCOUNTRY CAMPSITES: Established reservable sites that help protect fragile ecosystems from casual dispersed camping

BETA: Inside information about a hike. For example, Washington Trails Association has great online beta with its current trip reports.

CAIRN: A small stack of rocks marking a trail when the route is confusing

CAT HOLE: A small hole dug 6 to 8 inches deep to bury human waste

GPS: Global Positioning System, a constellation of satellites run by the US military to aid in navigation

POTABLE WATER: Water safe to drink without purifying

PRIMITIVE CAMPGROUND: Campgrounds with few amenities like restrooms, electricity, or potable water

SHOULDER SEASONS: The less crowded seasons before or just after the prime time for a sport or activity, typically early spring and late fall

TOPOGRAPHICAL MAP: Shows elevation change and contours, roads, and bodies of water

WALK-IN CAMPSITES: Campsites located a short walk from the campground parking lot

Winter Camping Tips and Tricks

Whether car camping or backpacking in winter, you'll have solitude, a breathtaking snowy landscape, the long night sky full of stars, and the glow of a campfire for an evening of storytelling. Always check the weather conditions and forecast to avoid impending storms, and give someone your location and estimated time of return. The following tips will help make winter camping a safe and enjoyable experience.

- Dress in layers: close-fitting synthetic base layer (no cotton!) to hold in body heat, next a down jacket, and over that a weatherproof shell. Hike in waterproof or insulated boots with boot liners and bring snowshoes for moving through deep snow.
- Set up your campsite in a protected forested area that offers shelter from blowing snow and cold winds. Pack down the snow before setting up the tent; packed snow is a better insulator than loose.
- Bring a sleeping bag that is rated for winter temperatures, or add a sleep sack liner (or two) to your old bag. Lay your sleeping pad on a closed-cell foam pad or a yoga mat. The body loses more heat to the ground than to the air.
- Place a hot water bottle at your feet in your sleeping bag.
- Place tomorrow's clothes, socks, and boot liners in the sleeping bag with you at night to keep them dry and warm; do the same with battery-operated devices to keep the batteries functioning normally.
- Vent the tent at night by unzipping the tent flap a few inches to reduce condensation inside.
- Don't postpone that middle-of-the-night pee; it burns precious calories needed to stay warm and will keep you awake. If you choose to stay in the tent, use a bottle with a lid, or buy a product made for this purpose.
- Remove the iced condensation from the inner walls of the tent in the morning before it melts and gets your gear wet.
- Always sit on an insulated pad in the snow to conserve body heat.
- Place water bottles upside down in snow. The snow is an insulator that slows ice formation, and the water will freeze at the bottom, leaving the top liquid.
- Bring plenty of hand warmers and use them in coat pockets, sleeping bags, and boots.

COMMON GEOLOGICAL FIELD TERMS

ALPINE ZONE: The area typically near the tops of tall peaks where the wind is strong and the soil too thin for trees or other large plants to grow. Local weather patterns can change the elevation of alpine zones within a region.

BASALT: A type of rock that rock climbers seek for its fine-grained structure. Basalt makes up about 90 percent of the earth's volcanic rock.

BUTTE: An isolated hill or mountain with a flat top rising above the surrounding region. Mesas are just big buttes.

CALDERA: A large crater formed when a volcano erupts and the center collapses. Crater Lake is a caldera.

CANYON: A deep gorge, typically with a river running through it.

CIRQUE: A horseshoe-shaped basin, circled by mountains, that is formed by glaciers.

COLUMNAR BASALT: Massive vertically standing basalt columns resulting from the cooling and uniform cracking of a previous and unusually thick basaltic lava flow.

CRATER: A bowl-shaped depression produced by a volcanic explosion or activity.

ERRATIC: A rock transported by glaciers that differs from the native rocks around it.

FAULT: A deep crack or fracture in the earth's surface. Movement along fault lines can cause earthquakes.

GLACIER SNOUT: The end of a glacier, also called a toe.

HANGING VALLEY: An open-ended valley lying above a typically larger valley. A river or stream often runs through the opening, down a cliff or steep wall, and forms a waterfall as it drops to the bigger valley below.

LAHAR: A debris or mudflow of water and volcanic ash emitted from a volcanic explosion.

MORAINE: Rocks and debris left behind as a glacier melts.

SADDLE: A ridge between two peaks.

SUBDUCTION: The movement of the edge of one of the earth's crustal plates forced below the edge of another.

TALUS OR SCREE FIELDS: A collection of broken rocks that have fallen from cliff faces to the base of crags, volcanoes, or mountains. These loose deposits can be tricky to keep your footing on and navigate, and are common in the Pacific Northwest.

TARN: A small mountain lake or pool typically found in a cirque.

VENT: An opening in a volcano where lava, gases, and rock erupt.

SHINRIN-YOKU, OR FOREST BATHING

Forest bathing is not swimming in a river beside a forest. It's not a naked dip in a lake. Shinrin-yoku, or forest bathing, was developed in Japan in the 1980s and has health benefits that scientific studies have backed up. Time spent meandering in a forest causes blood pressure to drop and cortisol levels to plummet, and helps move stress into a state of alert calm. In addition, there's growing scientific evidence that blood sugar levels in diabetics decrease and stabilize with time spent in the forest, but here's the trick: shinrin-yoku is connecting with nature slowly and deliberately. Forest bathing is a portal for the senses as you pay attention to the sounds of the forest, the pungent crush of pine needles, the feel of cold creek water on fingertips. Leave the electronic devices at home and take photos with your mind. Find a place in nature—a park, a forest, a creek, or a river—and allow the senses to be your guide with *no end goal or destination*. This is not your typical hike. Follow your nose, your ears, or your eyes, and most importantly take your time. Feel the texture of bark, throw rocks into water and watch the ripples, listen to the birds flitting and calling through the canopy. You're not going anywhere. You're taking in a powerful antidote to a stressful indoor life.

Hot Springs Etiquette

There are basically three kinds of hot springs: ones that may take a hike to reach—they're free, and you can soak in them naked; ones that are overseen by a concessionaire or private owner; and ones that have been developed, charge fees, and ban nudity. Soaking in a wilderness hot spring is a sublime experience and not the place for boisterous horseplay or drunken partying, particularly when you are sharing it with others. Here's the code:

- If you are at a public hot spring with a parking lot and a fee, families will be there and everyone will be wearing swimsuits. If you are at a hike-in hot spring, soakers will likely be nude, but not always, especially if it is a popular spot with people waiting for their turn. Bring a swimsuit just in case.
- Leave no trace! The biggest issues with hot springs are the garbage, beer cans, human waste, and toilet paper that surround them, making the sublime sleazy. Bring a plastic bag to pack out garbage.
- Respect the quiet of a good soak. Use movie-theater voices when speaking.
- If others are waiting, don't hog the hot spring for hours. If you are waiting, don't stand around sighing in full view of those in the water.
- If you are at a remote hot spring, check the temperature before entering to avoid burns.
- No dogs, even if the hike is designated "dog friendly." A lunging, panting pet does not create the best ambience.
- Hot springs are not baths; don't soap up or wash your hair. Ideally, you're clean before you get in to avoid cross-contamination and introducing pathogens.
- Drink plenty of water! It's easy to get dehydrated while soaking.

Hipcamp

This online alternative lodging company has a wide and eclectic offering of privately-owned tepees, cabins, treehouses, yurts, trailers, or simply places to pitch a tent. The company focuses on outdoor stays, with the owner often setting up activities to enhance your stay. Filter your search by location (for example, mountains), nearby activities (hiking, fishing, cycling, etc.), type of accommodation, and desired amenities. With parks and campgrounds increasingly more crowded, Hipcamp offers fun last-minute places to camp or glamp with an easy-to-use online booking system. *hipcamp.com*

INK PENS OR MARKERS

WATERCOLOR PAINTBRUSHES

SMALL CONTAINER
FOR WATER

PENCILS AND SHARPENER

IDENTIFICATION
GUIDE

WATERCOLOR TRAVEL SET

Art in the Mountains: A Nature Sketch Journal

To enrich your experience in the mountains, bring a sketch pad, a few fine-tip permanent pens or a pencil, and a portable watercolor set in your backpack. A sketch journal is not just for artists. Observing and drawing the overlooked details of nature—boulders set in a river, the texture of bark—slows you down, focuses attention, and draws you deeper into the microcosm of the wilderness. Pair the sketches with notes, observations, the date, and the place. Sketching in nature is an exceptional activity for all ages—and you don't need formal training!

SKETCHBOOK OR
DRAWING PAD

Dogs on the Trail

The Pacific Northwest has an abundance of dog-friendly trails, and there are a few rules all owners need to know (and if you don't think your dog can follow them, leave your pet at home).

- Your dog must be under control and on a leash at all times. Wildlife is vulnerable.
- When meeting other hikers, dog and owner should step well off the trail to allow others to pass.
- Horses can spook easily, and it's important not only to yield to them on the trail, but to keep your dog calm and quiet as well.
- Don't assume other dogs on the trail are friendly. Leash yours when approached by other canines.
- Leave no trace! Always, *always* hike with a poop bag and do not leave it on the side of the trail to retrieve "later." Alternately, if you are on a multiday hike, you can place the business in a composting latrine (if available) or bury it 6 inches deep.
- Don't use retractable leashes on the trail. Violent yanks can cause burns and cuts to both dog and human, and they encourage pulling over walking peacefully beside you.
- Stay on the main trail; don't cut switchbacks or take shortcuts.
- Buy a doggie backpack so your pet can carry their own food and poop bags. It's a visual signal to other hikers that yours is a seasoned trekker.

How to Poop in the Woods

Yes, there's a right and a wrong way to do it! Badly buried human waste is one of the most common types of pollution found in the wilderness. The right way: find a spot with soft soil, if possible 200 feet from water sources, campsites, and trails. Dig the hole at least 6 inches deep, setting the dirt to the side to cover your business afterward. Place all used toilet paper in a ziplock bag and pack it out. Pour a little water into the hole and stir with a stick. This simple step dramatically speeds up the decomposing process. Fill the hole with dirt. That's it! For women hikers who must wipe after peeing, buy a Kula Cloth (*kulacloth.com*). It's a small, colorful cloth with antimicrobial fabric on one side and waterproof fabric on the other, and it snaps to the backpack for easy access.

HOW TO RAISE A HIKER

A love of the outdoors is one of the greatest gifts parents can give their children, and it begins when they are young.

- Start early! Carry your infant in a pack or wrap, and progress to short forays on the trail when they learn to walk.
- Shoe them in comfortable footwear. Outdoor moccasins are especially comfortable for little hikers. Buy a one-piece waterproof rainsuit so they'll stay warm and dry in all seasons.
- Children can carry their own little backpack with cool tools, like a headlamp, compass, or walkie-talkie, in addition to water, snacks, and an extra layer.
- Embrace their pace! Walk at your child's speed. Support detours, investigations, and curiosity. Allow them to play with sticks and rocks and splash through mud puddles.
- Hike with friends who have children of mixed ages. Kids do better with peers and older kids they'll want to keep up with. Check out the website hikeitbaby.com to find hikes and connect with other families in your region.
- To begin, choose a trail that is wide enough to hold hands side by side and well defined enough that the kids can race ahead if they want to. Preferably it features a creek, a lake, or a waterfall at the end. Short loop trails are also a good option.
- Carry a first aid kit with bandages, sanitizing wipes, insect repellent, and sunscreen.
- Place a whistle in their backpack for them to blow if they get lost.
- Bring water and snacks, an extra diaper, hand wipes, and dried fruit for low blood sugar crashes.
- Teach trail etiquette. Say hello to passing hikers; don't take shortcuts on the trail. If your child needs to poop, teach her how to do it properly (see page 28).
- At bedtime after your hike, recap the adventure: what you saw, the narrow misses, and their speed or strength on the trail. This is a quiet but powerful tool of affirmation.

ALPINE LAKES WILDERNESS AREA, WASHINGTON

Play It Safe

One draw of the outdoors is its wild setting that will ask more of you—more awareness, more mindfulness. Read on to prevent mishaps or get out of them safely.

Mountain First Aid Kit

Pack a first aid kit to cover the most common hiking injuries and illnesses. Even better, take a class in wilderness first aid. You can buy a premade kit or tailor-make your own that could include an EpiPen, for example, if you are allergic to bees. Here are the basics:

- Needle, tweezers, and/or duct tape to remove splinters and stickers. Wind duct tape around a water bottle for easy storage.
- Alcohol wipes
- Antibacterial ointment
- Gauze pads
- Bandages
- Butterfly bandages and/or superglue for cuts
- Blister kit (see Blisters 101, below)
- Insect sting/itch ointment
- Antihistamine for allergic reactions
- Ibuprofen

If you have room, these are also good to have: SAM (structural, aluminum, malleable) splint, elastic wrap, an antidiarrheal medicine, hand sanitizer, emergency space blanket.

Blisters 101

Blisters can reduce a lovely walk in the woods to a painful crawl. They're the most common hiking injury, caused by repeated friction against the skin and exacerbated by heat and moisture—wet skin is softer and more vulnerable. To prevent blisters, you need well-fitted footwear, dry socks (no cotton; they hold moisture) or a liner inside the socks, and *immediate* attention to the start of a hot spot. Cover it with a padded blister bandage,

ANIMAL TRACKS

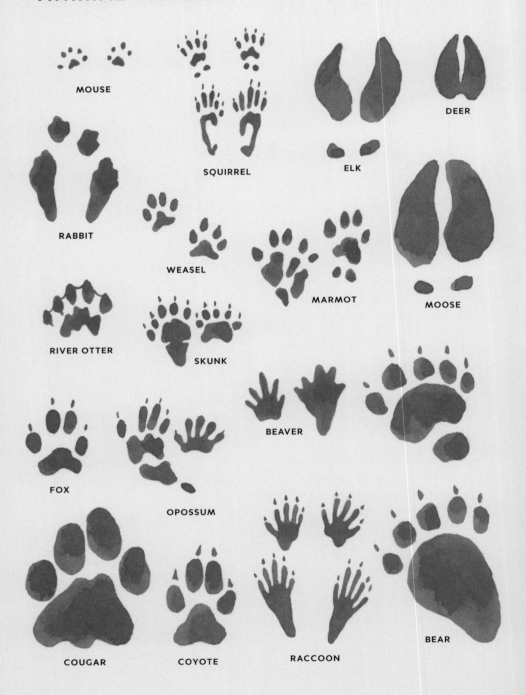

MOUSE

SQUIRREL

ELK

DEER

RABBIT

WEASEL

MARMOT

MOOSE

RIVER OTTER

SKUNK

FOX

OPOSSUM

BEAVER

COUGAR

COYOTE

RACCOON

BEAR

a piece of moleskin, or even a short length of tape—surgical paper tape or duct tape will work. Pausing to cover a hot spot can save you days of agony. If a blister has formed fluid, try not to pop it; it helps to protect and heal damaged skin. If the blister is large or already popped, prevent infection by cleaning it with soap and water or an alcohol wipe, then apply antibiotic ointment and a donut-shaped piece of moleskin to fit over the blister. If you're on the trail with several days of hiking ahead of you, keep the blister well protected with moleskin, wear dry socks, and address any additional hot spots quickly.

Make a blister kit by packing: moleskin, surgical paper tape, antibiotic ointment, blister-specific bandages, and alcohol wipes.

The Importance of Staying Hydrated

Water is vital to health, and it's essential to stay hydrated, particularly when spending time outdoors. There are many benefits to a well-hydrated body, including lubricated joints, regulated body temperature, and improved physical performance when you are out on the trails. To stay hydrated:

- Drink a liter of water before heading out, especially in warmer months.
- Plan on drinking a liter of water per hour on strenuous hikes in summer. Water is heavy! Map out water sources to filter along the route.
- Hydrate often in smaller amounts rather than taking less frequent large gulps. Use a hydration reservoir system for easy access to water as you hike.
- Drink more water when you are at higher altitudes.
- When you're thirsty, you're already dehydrated. Drink water in camp at breakfast before heading out.
- Symptoms of dehydration include headache, dry mouth, fatigue, dizziness, and nausea. When moderate dehydration occurs, get out of direct sunlight, cool yourself with a wet bandana, and sip water. When ready to move on, go slow, drinking often.

What to Do If You Get Lost

Getting lost on a wilderness hike can happen to even the most experienced hiker. The leading cause is going off trail. You lose the trail as it fades out, or take a shortcut or a wrong turn, and suddenly you've got the sinking feeling you're off course. The best prevention to getting lost is preparation. *Always* leave a trip plan and estimated time of return with a friend or relative. Even on day hikes, carry the 10 Essentials (see page 15). Keep them stored together in a ziplock bag at home, and when you're ready to hike, throw it in your backpack. Then add the map of your route and, more importantly, know how to read the contours: know what is a mountain, a valley, a ridge. Most beginners and even some seasoned hikers can't read a topo map correctly and it is a valuable skill. The Mountaineers offer an excellent basic navigation course (*mountaineers.org/blog/courses -activities/navigation*). Before leaving, download your map on your GPS, if you have one, and carry a paper map as a backup. On your GPS mark the car or trailhead as a waypoint before starting out. Track landscape features on the map as you hike for reference. If you do end up getting lost, the big question is whether to stay put until someone finds you, or find your own way back to familiar territory. If you haven't given someone your trip plan and estimated time of return, it may be best to find your own way out unless you are with children or the elderly, or you are a novice hiker: then stay put. This reduces your chance of getting injured or more lost, but it will add time to resolving a bad situation.

If you stay put:

- Find an open place to wait with sight lines in all directions.
- Yell or use a whistle at regular intervals.
- Form the letters "SOS" or the word "HELP" with rocks or downed branches in a clearing for rescuers searching by plane or helicopter.
- Build a fire (a lighter is one of the 10 Essentials) and place green plants or branches on it to create smoke. Do this only if you are able to control it and not start a wildfire.
- Hang colorful clothing or items from tree branches.
- Build a shelter, fill your water bottle if possible, and build a fire to stay warm if it looks like you'll be overnighting.

A successful self-rescue can shorten your time in the wilderness, but you risk making the situation worse if you launch yourself in the wrong direction. This is where a GPS or compass (one of the 10 Essentials) will help guide you. To increase the chances of finding your way back:

- Check your map and look for any recognizable landmarks—a mountain, a creek, or a river, for example—then orient yourself to the right direction.
- Avoid walking in circles, which is a common mistake; trust your compass or GPS.
- Climb to higher ground for an elevated view of the landscape or for possible cell phone coverage.
- Consider following a descending creek or river if you are lost without navigational aids. Flowing water will follow low ground and often bring you to a lake, a road, or a settlement. Simply going downhill can eventually lead you out to civilization.

Mosquito Control Tips

Camping in the great outdoors means you are sure to encounter mosquitoes during the summer months. Here's a guide to help you enjoy your time around the campfire.

- Avon's Skin So Soft bath oil is a great deterrent when rubbed on exposed skin. Start with the bath oil, and if the mosquitoes persist, move on to a bug spray with DEET, a powerful repellent.
- Cover up: wear long sleeves and pants when in camp. Avoid wearing dark clothing and the color blue. Studies have shown mosquitoes are attracted to blue. When the bugs are bad, wear a mosquito net that fits over a hat.
- Light a few mosquito repellent coils or citronella candles around camp.
- Light a campfire when allowed; mosquitoes tend to avoid smoke.
- When car camping, enjoy cocktail hour inside a screen room (a tent made of bug netting). They're relatively inexpensive and many are sized to fit over a picnic table.
- When hiking in the mountains during mosquito season, especially around alpine lakes, use a combination of permethrin on your clothing and 30 percent DEET on exposed skin for full protection.

POISONOUS PLANTS

WESTERN POISON IVY: Poison ivy contains a powerful oily sap called urushiol, which causes a blistered rash. It grows in a wide variety of habitats but is mostly found in shady forests as a low-growing vine. It emerges in spring and remains toxic throughout the growing season.

PACIFIC POISON OAK: Growing as a vine in damp shady areas and as a small shrub in sunnier sites, poison oak also contains urushiol, which causes a blistered rash. The oil can be spread to humans on the fur of their dogs. Like poison ivy, it emerges in spring and remains toxic throughout the growing season.

POISON SUMAC: The plant grows as a shrub or small tree in marshy areas. Contact with the leaves causes a rash similar to poison ivy and poison oak, to which it is related, and is to be avoided when the leaves emerge in spring.

POISON HEMLOCK: Considered a noxious weed, it grows 2 to 10 feet tall where forest has been cleared and in open sunny areas in fields, vacant lots, and roadsides. Ingesting even a small amount can kill humans and animals. Poison hemlock first appears in the spring.

STINGING NETTLE: The hairs along its leaves sting the skin and raise bumps. Found in damp soils along streams and meadows, stinging nettles emerge in May and can last into August or until first frost.

MEADOW DEATH CAMAS: All fresh parts are poisonous to livestock and humans. The cream-colored flowers grow on a 6- to 18-inch stalk in wet meadows. The death camas generally flowers in April and May at lower elevations and in late June and July at higher altitudes.

Wildfires 101

Wildfires have been increasing in size, intensity, and frequency over the years for many reasons, including climate change and past forestry management practices. It's important to be prepared for the possibility of a fire when heading to the mountains during the fire season. Wildfires are unpredictable and can spring up seemingly from nowhere. Arm yourself with information before you go by checking all currently burning major wildfires and checking the air quality for haze and smoke particulates. *inciweb.nwcg.gov; airnow.gov*

- Even if your hike looks clear, have a plan B and map out escape routes and safety zones such as large bodies of water. Choose routes with multiple trails and roads out of the area you plan to hike in.
- Lightning and high winds are a recipe for wildfire disaster; check the weather forecast, including thunderstorm and wind predictions, before hiking.
- If you see nearby smoke or flames, note the GPS coordinates, leave the area as quickly as possible, and immediately call 911 or notify the local ranger station with the location.
- If the fire is near, evacuate the area to tracts with less brush and timber, such as roads and rock fields. Avoid canyons and saddles, as they act as chimneys and draw the fire.
- Don't travel uphill—heat and flames rise.
- Flatter terrain is safer to shelter in; look for swampy areas, shallow creeks, and lakes.
- You can't outrun a fire, and if it is imminently close, yank up grass and shrubs to create an area around you with as little fire fuel as possible, dig a depression in the center, cover yourself with dirt, and lie facedown with your feet toward the flames.
- If you are near a water source, shelter there only if there is no overhanging foliage that could catch fire.
- Stay low to the ground when making your way out; the air will be better.

How to Drive on Icy Roads

Skiing, sledding, and snowshoeing will entice you outdoors on an otherwise dreary winter day, but getting there often means driving on icy roads. If you're in a terrifying skid toward a guardrail, the answer is counterintuitive. The typical first reaction is to slam on the brakes and steer sharply away from impact, but those are the worst things you can do. If you begin to skid, do *not* brake. This urge is difficult to overcome, but in fact sometimes the best move is to take your foot off the brake and apply a little power *into* the skid to regain steering control. This action pulls a front-wheel-drive car back into line and moves weight onto the rear wheels to help them regain grip, allowing you to pull out of the skid. Invest in snow tires, but always carry chains, which are required in many mountain regions featured in this book. Practice putting the chains on at home before leaving, and for safety's sake pull over at a designated chain-up area to put them on.

Sno-Parks 101

The number of people using Sno-Parks for winter recreation is growing. Here's what you need to know:

- Many Sno-Parks will close their parking lots when they are filled, and parking on the side of a highway or road is dangerous and not allowed. Plan to arrive early, especially on holidays and weekends.
- Save time and money by purchasing an annual permit instead of daily ones. In addition, in Washington, you will also need a special groomed trail permit, for all groomed Sno-Park trails whether you use them or not, available online. *epermits.parks.wa.gov* (Washington); *oregon.gov/odot/dmv* (Oregon)
- Cars and trucks are prohibited on all trails and forest roads within the Sno-Park.
- On groomed trails, snowshoers must walk on the side to stay off ski tracks; skiers and snowshoers must yield to snowmobilers and dog teams.

Bear Safety

Autumn is a splendid time to hike, but it's also the time that bears are filling their bellies with blueberries before winter, and both blueberries and bears can be plentiful in the mountains in the fall. While encountering a bear on the trail can be alarming, attacks on humans are rare, and most bears will avoid you if they hear you coming. When you know bears are near, make noise: whistle, clap, and carry on loud conversations. The two main rules when hiking in bear country are to keep your distance and to not surprise the bear. Hiking in groups helps because you're noisier and more intimidating, giving the bear a chance to leave the area on its own. Bear spray is a good deterrent used when the bear is *downwind*; otherwise, you'll be the one to get a face full of hot pepper spray.

BLACK BEAR

MOUNTAIN WILDLIFE

GRAY JAY

STELLER'S JAY

MOUNTAIN GOAT

NORTHERN SPOTTED OWL

MARMOT

RUFOUS HUMMINGBIRD

PACIFIC FISHER

COYOTE

FOX

MOOSE

ELK

DEER

OLYMPIC MOUNTAINS, WASHINGTON

PART 2

THE COAST RANGE

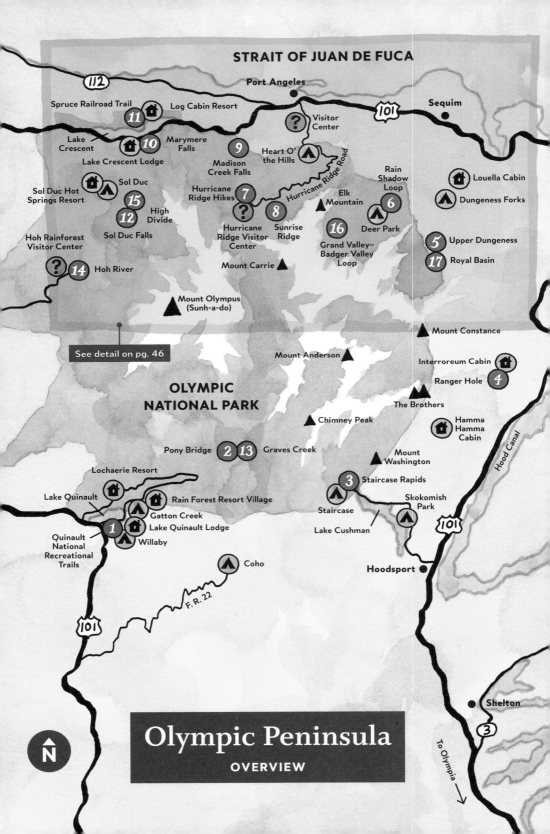

STRAIT OF JUAN DE FUCA

Port Angeles

Sequim

112

101

Spruce Railroad Trail
11 Log Cabin Resort

10 Lake Crescent

Lake Crescent Lodge

Marymere Falls

9 Madison Creek Falls

Heart O' the Hills

? Visitor Center

Hurricane Ridge Road

Louella Cabin

Dungeness Forks

Rain Shadow Loop

Sol Duc Hot Springs Resort
Sol Duc
15
12
High Divide
Sol Duc Falls

Hurricane Ridge Hikes **7**

? Hurricane Ridge Visitor Center

8 Sunrise Ridge

Elk Mountain

6 Deer Park

5 Upper Dungeness

17 Royal Basin

16 Grand Valley–Badger Valley Loop

Hoh Rainforest Visitor Center

? **14** Hoh River

Mount Carrie

Mount Olympus (Sunh-a-do)

See detail on pg. 46

OLYMPIC NATIONAL PARK

Mount Anderson

Mount Constance

Interroreum Cabin

4 Ranger Hole

The Brothers

Hamma Hamma Cabin

Chimney Peak

Pony Bridge **2** **13** Graves Creek

Mount Washington

Lochaerie Resort

Lake Quinault

Rain Forest Resort Village

Gatton Creek

1 Lake Quinault Lodge

Willaby

Quinault National Recreational Trails

3 Staircase Rapids

Staircase

Skokomish Park

Lake Cushman

101

Hood Canal

Coho

F.R. 22

101

Hoodsport

Shelton

3

N

To Olympia

Olympic Peninsula
OVERVIEW

Olympic Peninsula, Washington

The Olympic Mountains began in the sea. Between 18 and 57 million years ago, the Juan de Fuca Plate in the Pacific Ocean smashed into and was forced under (subducted) the North American Plate, which scraped off masses of rock onto the continent as it moved. Over millions of years, these masses were eroded by glaciers, water, and wind to create the valleys and jagged peaks of the Olympic Mountains, with Mount Olympus reigning tall in the center of the peninsula. The original Native American name for Mount Olympus is the Duwamish word Sunh-a-do, with the meaning unknown.

The Olympic Mountains are part of the Pacific Coast Range, which runs for over a thousand miles down the western coasts of British Columbia, Washington, Oregon, and Northern California. Bordered by the Pacific Ocean to the west, these peaks are separated from the Cascade Range by wide lowlands to the east—the Interior Plateau in British Columbia, the Puget Sound lowlands in Washington, and the Willamette Valley in Oregon.

The Olympics are surrounded by the Pacific Ocean to the west, Hood Canal to the east, and the Strait of Juan de Fuca to the north, making the peninsula almost island-like. Sunh-a-do is only 35 miles from the Pacific Ocean, and at 7,930 feet it's considered one of the steepest reliefs in the country from base to summit.

The climate in the Olympics is defined by the prevailing westerly winds from the Gulf of Alaska, which dump heavy rain on the western slopes—more than 150 inches annually in places—before easing off in the rain shadow of the leeward flanks of the mountains. Over the centuries the deluge of rain established rain forests of towering Douglas fir, western red cedar, and Sitka spruce, with an Eden of moss and ferns at their feet. Hiking through this cathedral of trees is a journey of awe and wonder. The wet, cool, and moderate climate of the rain forest in the Olympics encourages such an abundance and variety of plants that naturalist Roger Tory Peterson claimed it contained "the greatest weight of living matter per acre in the world," with nearly every inch of land filled. This vast richness decomposes slowly, leaving a fertile vegetation base and very little empty ground.

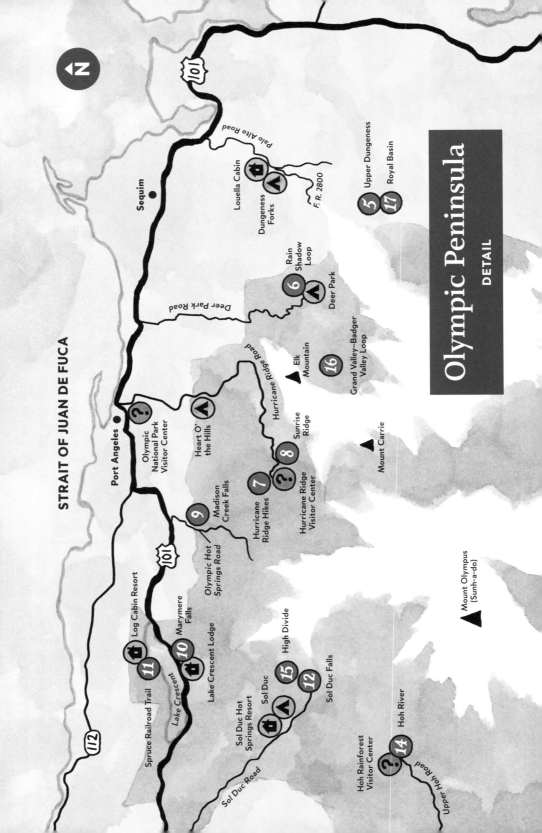

Olympic Peninsula

DETAIL

STRAIT OF JUAN DE FUCA

Port Angeles

Sequim

112

101

101

Mount Olympus
(Sunh-a-do)

Mount Carrie

Elk Mountain

Spruce Railroad Trail

Lake Crescent

Log Cabin Resort

Lake Crescent Lodge

Marymere Falls

Sol Duc Road

Sol Duc Hot Springs Resort

Sol Duc

High Divide

Sol Duc Falls

Hoh Rainforest Visitor Center

Upper Hoh Road

Hoh River

Olympic Hot Springs Road

Madison Creek Falls

Olympic National Park Visitor Center

Heart O' the Hills

Hurricane Ridge Hikes

Hurricane Ridge Road

Sunrise Ridge

Hurricane Ridge Visitor Center

Deer Park Road

Rain Shadow Loop

Deer Park

Grand Valley–Badger Valley Loop

Palo Alto Road

Louella Cabin

Dungeness Forks

F. R. 2800

Upper Dungeness

Royal Basin

5 17 6 16 ? 7 8 9 ? 15 12 10 11 ? 14

The long human history in the Olympic Range began at least 10,000 years ago with hunter-gatherer groups who explored and hunted over the entire peninsula. In 1993 a Florida family hiking near Hurricane Ridge found a piece of woven material near a receding snowfield. It was a fragment of a 2,900-year-old basket, evidence of the original residents who lived there. Today eight tribes maintain a connection to the Olympic Peninsula: Makah, Hoh, Quinault, Skokomish, Quileute, Port Gamble S'Klallam, Jamestown S'Klallam, and Lower Elwha Klallam.

Your first stop before heading into the Olympic Mountains should be the Olympic National Park Visitor Center on the way to Hurricane Ridge. The staff can help with trip planning, current trail conditions, and the weather forecast. If you are overnighting in the backcountry, pick up the mandatory wilderness camping permits and bear canisters here. Roughly half the permits are for advance reservation only, and the other half are first come, first served at the visitor center. While you're there, buy a map of your route. Paper maps give you the big picture, offer alternative routes, and take up little space.

Get Away

CAMPGROUNDS ▲

Unless otherwise noted, all campgrounds in the Olympic National Park are first come, first served.

Willaby

This is the most popular campground on Lake Quinault, with easy access to trailheads for exploring the waterfall-laced Quinault River valley. Reservations accepted; closed in winter.

Gatton Creek ♿

This small, idyllic campground is on the shores of Lake Quinault with 5 walk-in sites. Closed in winter.

Coho ♿

The campground is located on the western shore of Wynoochee Lake, where you can swim, boat, and fish. You can make reservations for the 46 sites and there are nearby showers and potable water. Closed in winter.

Sol Duc ♿

There are many reasons to camp here, including the proximity to Sol Duc Hot Springs, the nearby trailheads into the heart of the mountains, and the wide path and beautiful walk to Sol Duc Falls. It's one of the few campgrounds that takes reservations. Closed in winter.

Heart O' the Hills ♿

This is the closest car campground to Hurricane Ridge. Its proximity to Port Angeles means that the 106 sites fill quickly during peak season. Open year-round.

Deer Park ♿

The 18-mile road to the campground is steep and narrow, but this is one of my favorite campsites in the Olympic Mountains, especially during a full moon or meteor showers—bring a camp chair to watch the night sky. Bring water, too, as there is none at the campground. Several trailheads for longer hikes leave from the campground, including Three Forks, Slab Camp, and Obstruction Point. Closed from late fall to snowmelt, usually in late spring.

Staircase ♿

Sitting on the bank of the North Fork of the Skokomish River, the campground is close to Lake Cushman. There are miles of hiking trails off the beaten path here, and the fishing is good. The 51 sites have nearby restrooms and potable water. Open in winter with no water or restrooms available.

Skokomish Park

There are two campgrounds, North and South; the South has RV hookups and an outdoor theater for movie night and educational talks. The campgrounds are located in a 600-acre park next to Lake Cushman with plenty of amenities, including showers, potable water, and a general store on-site. Reservations accepted; closed in winter.

CABINS AND LODGES 🏠

Lake Quinault Lodge ♿

Relax in front of the huge fireplace in the lobby of this historic place featured in the PBS series *Great Lodges of the National Parks*. Built in 1926 in the wild heart of the rain forest, the lodge has a grassy front lawn that sweeps down to Lake Quinault, where you can fish, paddle, or lounge by the shore. In winter, hike nearby trails into the rain forest, and return to dry clothes and a comfortable bed.

Rain Forest Resort Village ♿

The world's largest Sitka spruce tree grows on the resort's property, and it's a wonder to behold. The spruce is estimated to be nearly a thousand years old and stands 191 feet tall with a circumference of nearly 60 feet. The resort is just down the road from Lake Quinault Lodge and is a more affordable alternative. There are both motel rooms and cabins with gas fireplaces here, but no kitchens. Family friendly; open year-round.

Lochaerie Resort

Spring is my favorite time to visit the rain forest and hike along the Hoh River, and these Lake Quinault shore cabins are a delight to return to after chilly, damp walks. The 6 cabins were built in the 1920s to 1930s and have woodstoves, bathrooms, and kitchens. Canoes and kayaks are available to guests. Open year-round.

Sol Duc Hot Springs Resort ♿

The resort has three mineral hot springs of varying temperatures to relax and soak in. There's also a large freshwater pool and easy access to trails leading into the Sol Duc Valley (don't miss the hike to the falls!). There are 32 cabins that sleep up to four, RV sites, and a spa that offers massages. Reservations recommended in the summer months; closed in winter.

Lake Crescent Lodge ♿

The glassed-in porch, inviting lobby, and large fireplace fill this historic lodge with Old World charm. There's a restaurant on-site. Choose between cabins (reserve early for the Roosevelt Fireplace Cabins), a room in the lodge, or simple rooms in stand-alone buildings. Reservations recommended; closed in winter.

SOL DUC RIVER, WASHINGTON

Log Cabin Resort ♿

Situated on the shore of Lake Crescent, this resort offers multiple accommodations—from tent camping sites to a wide range of cabins with varying amenities. The resort also has boats and kayaks for rent. Log Cabin Resort is ideal for families or those who want a comfortable place to return to after a long day's hike. Closed in winter.

Louella Cabin

Built and maintained by the US Forest Service (USFS), the four-room cabin has many amenities—lights and electricity, a refrigerator, and a propane heater—but no potable water (bring your own) or bedding. Open year-round.

Interrorem Cabin

Located in the Duckabush Recreation Area, this charming peeled-log cabin was built in 1907 and is also run by the USFS. Potable water is available through a hand pump in the yard, and it's kept warm inside with a propane heater. There's no indoor plumbing or electricity, but that's more than compensated for by a beautiful setting in a verdant forest of hemlock and cedar. Open year-round by reservation.

Hamma Hamma Cabin

Another historic USFS cabin built in 1936 on Olympic National Forest land, this cabin is located near the Brothers and Mount Skokomish Wilderness areas. It sleeps up to six and has a bathroom, propane heater, and lights, but no potable water; you'll have to bring your own as well as sleeping linens. Available by reservation year-round.

Season of Green

DAY HIKES

1. Quinault National Recreation Trails ☺ ⚲ 🍂 🐾

- Northwest Forest Pass
- Easy
- 4–10 miles, depending on the loop
- 300 feet elevation gain
- 3–4 hours

The recreation trails offer 10 miles of interconnecting paths through an old-growth rain forest of monster trees. The wide, gently graded paths run along the shoreline of Lake Quinault, past multiple waterfalls. *wta.org/go-hiking/hikes/quinault-national-recreation-trails*

2. Quinault River Pony Bridge ☺ ⚲ ✿ 🍂 ♨

- America the Beautiful Pass
- Easy
- 4.8 miles round trip out and back
- 1,164 feet elevation gain
- 4–5 hours

This short and glorious day hike is on the way to the Enchanted Valley. Your destination is the picturesque Pony Bridge, which crosses the Quinault River 2.5 miles from the trailhead. Do this hike in winter and you may run across some of the largest elk herds in America. *alltrails.com*

3. Staircase Rapids ☺ ⚲

- America the Beautiful Pass
- Easy
- 2.2-mile loop
- 150 feet elevation gain
- 1–2 hours

This is a satisfying year-round hike near Lake Cushman leading through corridors of cedar, Douglas fir, and hemlock, with sections along the North Fork of Skokomish River. It's a great introductory hike for kids. *myolympicpark.com*

SOL DUC RIVER, WASHINGTON

4. Ranger Hole–Interrorem Nature Trail ☺ ⚲ 🐾

- Northwest Forest Pass
- Easy
- 2.1 miles round trip out and back
- 200 feet elevation gain
- 1–1.5 hours

If you're staying at the Interrorem cabin, you're in luck; the trailhead for this pleasant hike is in your backyard. There's also a short interpretive walk to help identify plants of the lowland forest as you hike. *wta.org*

5. Upper Dungeness ☺ ✿ 🍁 🐾

- Northwest Forest Pass
- Easy to moderate
- 6.8 miles round trip out and back
- 600 feet elevation gain
- 3–4 hours round trip out and back

The Dungeness River valley is a deep groove between drainages smack in the middle of the rain shadow of the Olympic Mountains, making it significantly drier than the rest of the Olympic Peninsula. It's the go-to hike when the weather is iffy, with a picturesque stroll along the river to Camp Handy, where there's a shelter for a picnic before you head back. *alltrails.com*

6. Rain Shadow Loop ☺ ⚲ ✿ ✨

- America the Beautiful Pass
- Easy
- 0.5-mile loop
- 170 feet elevation gain
- 1 hour

This short, enchanting hike starts high and climbs a mere 170 feet for 360-degree views from the top of Blue Mountain. On a clear day you'll see the Strait of Juan de Fuca, the Cascades, Vancouver Island, Dungeness Spit with its 5-mile sandbar, and so much more. There are postcard vistas in all directions, and the high alpine meadow is lit with wildflowers in July and August. The trailhead is a short drive from Deer Park campground. The road closes for the winter from October to May. *wta.org*

THE OLYMPIC RANGE

(AS SEEN FROM DOWNTOWN SEATTLE)

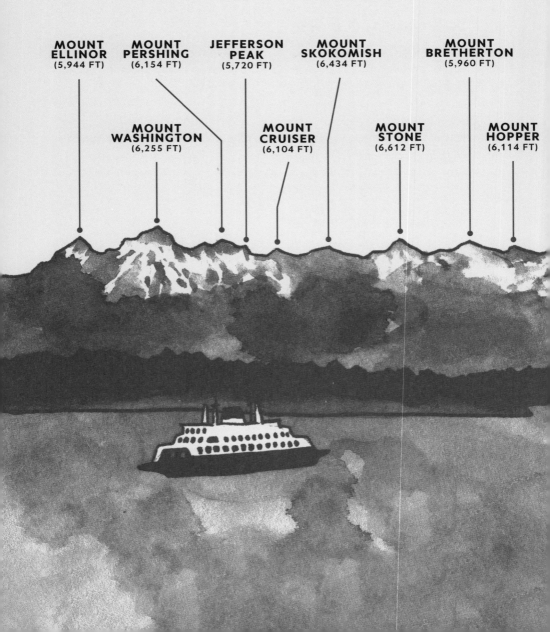

MOUNT
ELLINOR
(5,944 FT)

MOUNT
PERSHING
(6,154 FT)

JEFFERSON
PEAK
(5,720 FT)

MOUNT
SKOKOMISH
(6,434 FT)

MOUNT
BRETHERTON
(5,960 FT)

MOUNT
WASHINGTON
(6,255 FT)

MOUNT
CRUISER
(6,104 FT)

MOUNT
STONE
(6,612 FT)

MOUNT
HOPPER
(6,114 FT)

THE BROTHERS (6,866 FT)

MOUNT ANDERSON (7,321 FT)

MOUNT CONSTANCE (7,743 FT)

THE NEEDLES (7,650 FT)

ST. PETERS DOME (4,490 FT)

MOUNT JUPITER (5,701 FT)

WARRIOR PEAKS (7,300 FT)

7. Hurricane Ridge Visitor Center Trails

Hurricane Ridge Visitor Center offers the easiest access to the Olympic Mountains. At 5,242 feet you'll feel the majestic draw of the mountains, and many easy loops and trails leave from the center. Note that the 17-mile Hurricane Ridge Road is open in the winter season from Friday to Sunday, weather dependent. In winter all vehicles must carry chains. *nps.gov*

Big Meadow ✿ ☀ ♿

An easy, paved 0.25-mile traverse over open meadows. Wheelchair accessible with some assistance.

Cirque Rim ✿ ☀ ♿

An easy 0.5-mile paved trail, also wheelchair accessible with assistance.

High Ridge ✿ ☀

A partially paved 0.5-mile loop that climbs 250 feet to a dynamic view from Alpine Hill.

Hurricane Hill ✿ ☀

A popular 3-mile round-trip trail that ascends 700 feet to rolling views of the Olympic Mountains and the Strait of Juan de Fuca.

8. Sunrise Ridge ☺ ✿ ☀

- **Easy to moderate**
- **5.2 miles round trip out and back**
- **1100 feet elevation gain**
- **2–3 hours**

The Sunrise Ridge Trail is a delightful alternative to the often-crowded Hurricane Hill trail, and you're more likely to encounter wildlife, especially in the morning. An abundance of wildflowers bloom from midsummer to the end of August. At 2.6 miles this hike delivers you to the base of soaring Mount Angeles. *mountaineers.org*

9. Madison Creek Waterfalls ☺ ⚲ ♨ ⚵

- America the Beautiful Pass
- Easy
- 0.3 miles round trip out and back
- 40 feet elevation gain
- 5 minutes

This beautiful trail is on a paved path and accessible to all. The 76-foot-tall horsetail falls make a cinematic backdrop for a family photo. To expand your walk, the Olympic Hot Springs Road is closed to traffic beyond the trailhead parking lot and offers excellent paved stroller/bicycle/wheelchair access for 1 mile to a washout. *alltrails.com*

10. Marymere Falls ☺ ⚲ ♨

- America the Beautiful Pass
- Easy
- 1.8 miles round trip out and back
- 500 feet elevation gain
- 1.5–2 hours

The impressive two-stage plunge waterfall drops 119 feet, filling the air with the sound of cascading water. It's an easy hike with a wide, level trail except for the 500-foot climb to the viewing site at the end. After the hike, treat yourself to lunch at nearby Lake Crescent Lodge. *wta.org*

11. Spruce Railroad Trail ☺ ⚲

- America the Beautiful Pass
- Easy
- 8 miles round trip out and back
- 260 feet elevation gain
- 4 hours

The trail follows an historic railroad grade for 4 easy miles that make up a signature piece of the 130-mile-long Olympic Discovery Trail. After the first mile you'll come to Devil's Punchbowl, where there is a jump, if you dare, from low cliffs into the impossibly clear water of Crescent Lake. *protrails.com*

TYPES OF WATERFALLS

BLOCK: The falls drop in a wide sheet, usually wider than their height (think Niagara Falls).

SEGMENTED: Distinctly separate parallel flows of water drop over the same ledge side by side.

TIER: The water flows in multiple drops over several sections of the falls.

CHUTE: A high volume of water moves through a small canyon.

EPHEMERAL: These waterfalls flow only after a rain or a significant snowmelt.

PLUNGE: The falls drop and lose contact with the bedrock surface behind them.

HORSETAIL: The falls start narrow, then make contact with the rock surface behind them, causing the water to spray out from the original path in the shape of a horsetail.

PUNCHBOWL: This is a subtype of a plunge waterfall, where the falls drop in a constricted form and then spread out to a catch pool at the bottom.

FAN: Similar to a horsetail, the falls begin narrow, then spread horizontally as they drop, with generally less velocity of water than a horsetail, widening as they fall into a fan shape.

12. Sol Duc Falls ☺ ♀ 🍁 ♨

- America the Beautiful Pass
- Easy
- 1.6 miles round trip out and back
- 200 feet elevation gain
- 1–2 hours

The trail wanders through a beautiful old-growth forest, but the falls are the main attraction. When there's heavy spring runoff, the current of the Sol Duc River can split into as many as four channels of cascading water into a segmented plunge, making it one of the loveliest waterfalls on the Olympic Peninsula. *wta.org*

MULTIDAY BACKPACKING

13. Enchanted Valley from Graves Creek ✿ ⚞ 🍁 ☆ ♨

- America the Beautiful Pass, backcountry permit
- Moderate
- 26 miles round trip out and back
- 1700 feet elevation gain
- 13–15 hours

The Enchanted Valley is wild, beautiful, and home to resident herds of elk, black bear, and river otter. This is one of the rare hikes that take you deep into the Olympic Mountains with little elevation gain. The trail winds beside the East Fork of the Quinault River through ancient old-growth forests and past dozens of plunging waterfalls. There are many inviting campsites along the way, including at O'Neil Creek, 6.7 miles in, an easy place to camp or turn around for a shorter hike. There's a historic chalet in the valley that was once a mountain retreat for weary travelers but is now closed. Check out the world's largest western hemlock, nearly 28 feet in circumference, a short hike from the chalet. *protrails.com*

14. Hoh River Trail to Tom Creek Camp ☺ ☆

- America the Beautiful Pass, backcountry permit
- Easy
- 6 miles round trip out and back
- 600 feet elevation gain
- 3 hours

This hike covers the first 3 miles of the 17.5-mile Hoh River Trail, gently winding through the iconic Hoh Rain Forest and following the river for 3 miles to Tom Creek camp. During the shoulder seasons of spring and fall, it's an excellent first-time overnight hike ending at an enchanting campsite

SOL DUC FALLS, WASHINGTON

beside the Hoh River. At night in autumn listen for the high bugling of resident elk. It's truly a magical trip. *nps.gov*

15. High Divide Loop to 7 Lakes Basin ⚙ ✴ ♨

- America the Beautiful Pass, backcountry permit
- Moderate to difficult

- 18.2-mile loop
- 3,050 feet elevation gain
- 10–12 hours

Avid hikers arrive from all over the world to do this stunning hike, and it doesn't disappoint. You'll moan at the steep grade upward, but you'll never forget the vistas, the alpine meadows filled with wildflowers, the high ridge walks, and the inviting lakes to splash in after a day on the trail. The trail begins at the Sol Duc Falls trailhead. From there, do the loop clockwise or counterclockwise; either way you'll start with a climb. There are many backcountry campsites along the trail to tease you into spending several days exploring, but before hiking make backcountry permit reservations. Plan on at least one night beside a lake in the 7 Lakes Basin. *nps.gov*

16. Grand Valley–Badger Valley Loop ⚙ ✴

- America the Beautiful Pass, backcountry permit
- Moderate to difficult

- 8.4-mile loop
- 3,185 feet elevation gain
- 6–7 hours

This was one of my first overnight hikes in the Olympics, and many backpacking trips later, I still consider it one of my favorites. You could make this a day hike, but you'll want to linger at one of the lakes (Moose is my choice) and revel in the meadows. *alltrails.com*

17. Royal Basin ⚙ 🐾 ✴ ♨

- Northwest Forest Pass, backcountry permit
- Moderate to difficult

- 14.4 miles round trip out and back
- 2,650 feet elevation gain
- 8–10 hours

Wake up in paradise. This hike holds the best the Olympic Mountains have to offer: turquoise glacier-fed lakes, deep forest, and waterfalls. Meadows and formidable peaks surround your camp. A broad alpine valley cups Royal Lake, with several campsites on the west shore and more in the meadows behind it. The start of the hike along the Dungeness River is gentle, but the last several miles are steep with rugged grades that will make you sweat with a fully loaded backpack. Camp at the lake, and the next day continue up on the trail a short way to Royal Basin Falls—a spectacular segmented horsetail waterfall. Bring snow and ice footwear traction and poles if hiking early in the season or late in the fall; there's always the possibility of snow. *nps.gov*

EXPLORE MORE ADVENTURES

Soak It Up at a Hot Spring

Sol Duc Hot Springs Resort has three hot spring soaking pools and one freshwater pool. The mineral-rich water comes from snowmelt and rain mingling with hot gases seeping from cooling volcanic rocks deep below the earth's surface. You can use the hot springs for the day or stay at the resort in cabins, the lodge, an RV park, or the campground. There are excellent nearby hikes. Closed for the winter November through March. *olympicnationalparks.com*

Mountain Bike the Lower Big Quilcene

The Lower Big Quilcene is an easy to intermediate trail with little elevation gain. The track winds through tall evergreens as it follows the Lower Big Quilcene River. It's a good trail for beginners wanting to one-up their skills and a great ride in spring when other trails are snowbound. *trailforks.com*

Cycle the Olympic Discovery Trail

The Discovery Trail is worth a mention for its heroic bid to cross the peninsula in 130 miles from Port Townsend on Puget Sound to La Push on the Pacific side. Currently more than half of the trail is on nonmotorized paths that weave along rivers, beside Puget Sound, and into the ever-present kingdom of evergreens. The other half uses roads, but more nonmotorized sections are added every year. It's a wonderful way to explore the peninsula by bicycle. *olympicdiscoverytrail.org*

EDIBLE WILD MUSHROOMS

CHANTERELLE
MUSHROOM

FAIRY RING
MUSHROOM

MATSUTAKE
(PINE MUSHROOM)

LION'S MANE
MUSHROOM

BLACK MOREL
MUSHROOM

CHICKEN OF
THE WOODS

Forage for Mushrooms

The Olympic Peninsula is a mushroom wonderland. The combination of mild temperatures, abundant rainfall, and a rich forest floor of organic matter fosters a huge variety of culinary wild mushrooms, chanterelles among them. Not only are they delicious with their meaty texture and subtle but fruity taste, but they're also among the easiest to identify; however, to be safe, *always* go with an experienced guide if you are new to harvesting. Joining a mycological club, such as Puget Sound Mycological Society, is an excellent way to familiarize yourself with finding and identifying the edible mushrooms of the Pacific Northwest.

Count the Stars

At Hurricane Ridge the National Park Service (NPS) offers an astronomy program during summer months. The clear skies at this high elevation are far from urban light pollution and offer remarkable views of the stars. You'll join a master observer and use telescopes to discover nebulae, stars, the moon, and planets. *nps.gov*

Season of Snow

Before heading out, always check the weather forecast and current road conditions. *nps.gov/olym/planyourvisit/weather.htm; nps.gov/olym /planyourvisit/current-conditions.htm*

SNOWSHOE TRAILS

Guided Snowshoe Trips

Take a ranger-guided snowshoe walk at the Hurricane Ridge Visitor Center to learn more about the natural history of the Olympic Mountains. It's less than a mile and suitable for all ages, with snowshoes provided. The walks are offered on weekends from mid-December through March. There are also many other trails to snowshoe from Hurricane Ridge, with rentals available from the center. *nps.gov*

Forest Service Roads

One of the gifts of Olympic National Park is that there are few paved roads burrowing deep into its heart, but many Forest Service roads. These gravel roads are often closed in winter when snow accumulates, and many are gated, making marvelous easy-to-follow snowshoe lanes. They also have the advantages of being wider and having deeper snow than other trails that are more protected by the forest canopy. You may have to drive or walk down a road several miles to get to the snow. Visit the USFS website for a list of roads in the park and their current conditions. *fs.usda.gov*

DOWNHILL SKI AND SNOWBOARD TRIPS

Hurricane Ridge

One of the few downhill ski areas in a national park, this is small and family oriented with two rope tows and a Poma lift. Beginners trying skis for the first time outnumber bombing boarders, but the area has extensive backcountry access with plenty of steeps, bowls, and glades for experienced skiers and boarders willing to hike. The visitor center has a snack bar and a gear rental shop that caters to families. The lifts are open weekends only from early December to late March; the most up-to-date information on rates and hours can be found at *olympicnationalparks.com*.

EXPLORE MORE ADVENTURES

Tube the Ridge

The tubes are available for rent on-site (no other sledding devices allowed) in 1-hour increments. Then sip hot chocolate at the visitor center after a romp-filled afternoon.

Hike the Rain Forest

The Hoh Rain Forest is a magical place, and its cathedral of old-growth evergreens and the carpet of ferns and mosses absorb sound like a recording musician's dream. It rarely snows, and to hike it in winter—and yes, in the rain—is a walking meditation in green. Get good rain gear and rent a cozy cabin to return to. *nps.gov*

Go World-Class Steelhead Fishing

Steelhead are an anadromous stock of rainbow trout that swim from the sea to the fresh water of rivers to spawn. Steelhead eclipse rainbows in size and can grow up to 30 pounds in salt water before returning to the river. They are a prize, particularly to anglers who come from all over the world to the Olympic Peninsula in winter to fish for them. December and January are the best months for steelhead fishing. There are dozens of small owner-operated guiding services on the Olympic Peninsula with an insider's knowledge of fly-fishing patterns and locations. *wdfw.wa.gov/fishing/reports/creel/steelhead*

MOUNT BAKER, WASHINGTON

PART 3

THE WASHINGTON CASCADES

MOUNT BAKER NATIONAL FOREST, WASHINGTON

The Cascade Range
Yamakiasham Yaina

The Cascade Range climbs assertively from the wide lowlands that separate it from the Coast Range. Part of the Pacific Ring of Fire, the range stretches over 700 miles from the Fraser River in British Columbia to Lassen Peak in Northern California. It is braided with rivers, studded with volcanoes and glaciers, and drenched in lakes and waterfalls. Indigenous peoples who've lived in the Cascades for millennia call the Cascades Yamakiasham Yaina, or "Mountains of the Northern People." For early non-Native explorers, it was the abundant waterfalls that gave Yamakiasham Yaina their name "the Cascades," and there are hundreds, perhaps thousands, that are unmarked on any maps. But the volcanoes make the Cascade Range unique in North America. The range is almost entirely volcanic in origin, formed by similar geological forces that created the Olympic Peninsula: born from the sea millions of years ago off the coast as the oceanic Juan de Fuca Plate was subducted beneath the continental North American Plate. The collision scraped mountainous stacks of rocks from the Juan de Fuca Plate onto the continental plate creating the Cascades. Volcanoes were formed when the diving plate sliced into the scorching rocks of the asthenosphere, melting them into magma that boiled to the surface. It's a geological force that continues to uplift the range today as the Juan de Fuca Plate is dragged down into the earth's mantle. This force, along with the seismic activity that goes with it, is the reason the Puget Sound region is anticipating a major earthquake.

There are four types of volcanoes: cinder cones, lava domes, shield volcanoes, and stratovolcanoes, also known as composites because of their composed layers of hardened lava and pyroclastic flows. These flows form the soaring peaks, typically over 10,000 feet, that people envision when they think of volcanoes: steep sides, a pointed top, and a vent at the peak. Although the Cascade Range has all four types of volcano, the stratovolcanoes claim the skyline—with Mount Baker, Mount Rainier, Mount Hood, and Three Sisters among the many. This 700-mile chain of volcanoes is wildly imposing, active, and unpredictable. All recent volcanic eruptions in the continental USA occurred in the Cascades.

The climatic barrier of the Yamakiasham Yaina range divides the Pacific Northwest into the wet west side of the mountains and the dry east side. On the west side, massive winter storms can sweep in from the Pacific Ocean and drop nearly a thousand inches of snow at Mount Baker, whereas the rain shadow of the east side has places with near-desertlike conditions. Summers on the west side of the Cascades are glorious with mild temperatures and long periods of little or no rain, perfect for camping and hiking.

The waterfalls, volcanoes, turquoise alpine lakes, and sweeping valleys of the Yamakiasham Yaina are the iconic images of the outdoors, but the range is also replete with wildlife. Less than 3 hours from urban centers you may see black bears, coyotes, deer, marmots, elk, moose, and a wide variety of resident and migratory birds. Much of the Cascade Mountains are easily accessible from the nearby urban centers of Seattle and Portland, but that also means the campgrounds and trails can be crowded, particularly on weekends. If possible, plan your outings for midweek during the summer months and use the shoulder season of fall—September and October—to avoid the crowds.

VOLCANO TYPES

CINDER CONE

SHIELD VOLCANO

LAVA DOME

COMPOSITE VOLCANO
(STRATOVOLCANO)

MOUNT BAKER, WASHINGTON

Mount Baker, Washington

Kulshan

Mantled by snow and glaciers, Mount Baker rises 10,781 feet to dominate the skyline of the North Cascades. The Lummi Nation calls Mount Baker Kulshan, meaning "shot at the extreme end, or very point," likely referring to past fiery volcanic eruptions (not meaning "Great White Watcher," as it is often defined). Note that there are many other Native names for Mount Baker with multiple meanings.

Kulshan is a stratovolcano, rated the second most active volcano in the Cascade Range after Mount St. Helens, and on some cold, clear days you can see plumes of steam surging from fumaroles on Sherman Crater. It is one of the snowiest places on earth. In 1999, Kulshan set the world record for snowfall in a single season with 95 feet recorded. That year trenches were dug into the snow for moving the ski chairlifts up the mountain.

The 58-mile Mount Baker Scenic Highway (State Route 542) winds its way along the Nooksack River from Bellingham to the base of Mount Baker at Heather Meadows, a route studded with waterfalls and pullouts where you can pause and drink in the landscape. The last 2.7 miles of the road lead to Artist Point, open for only a few short months—generally from late July to the first substantial snowfall of the year, usually in late September. August and early September are prime visiting and hiking time in the Artist Point area. Even during summer months bring snow and ice footwear traction to traverse unexpected snowfields that haven't melted, and stop at the seasonally open Glacier Public Service Center on the way up SR 542 for maps, guides, and recreation passes for your adventures. The Kulshan region is remote, with little cell service and fewer lodging options and services than more developed mountain ranges. To access the southern portion of the Mount Baker district, take Highway 20 from the town of Burlington to Baker Lake Road, which in approximately 15 miles will bring you to Baker Lake. Highway 20 and SR 542 are the two main routes into this vast and majestic area.

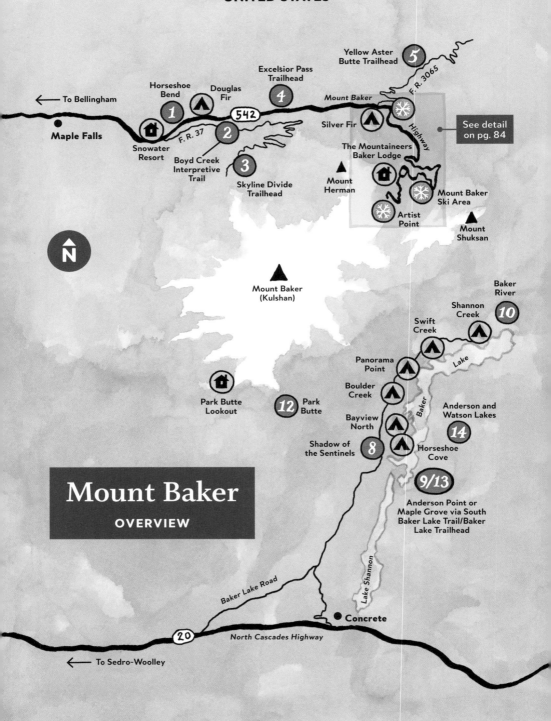

CANADA

UNITED STATES

Yellow Aster
Butte Trailhead **5**

F.R. 3065

← To Bellingham

Horseshoe
Bend **1**

Douglas
Fir

Excelsior Pass
Trailhead **4**

Mount Baker

Maple Falls

542

Snowater Resort

F.R. 37

2

Silver Fir

Boyd Creek
Interpretive
Trail

3

Skyline Divide
Trailhead

The Mountaineers
Baker Lodge

Mount
Herman

❄

Artist
Point

Highway

❄ Mount Baker
Ski Area

Mount
Shuksan

See detail
on pg. 84

N

Mount Baker
(Kulshan)

Baker
River

Shannon
Creek **10**

Swift
Creek

Panorama
Point

Lake

Park Butte
Lookout

12 Park
Butte

Boulder
Creek

Baker

Anderson and
Watson Lakes

14

Bayview
North

Shadow of
the Sentinels **8**

Horseshoe
Cove

9/13

Anderson Point or
Maple Grove via South
Baker Lake Trail/Baker
Lake Trailhead

Mount Baker

OVERVIEW

Lake Shannon

Baker Lake Road

Concrete

20

North Cascades Highway

← To Sedro-Woolley

Get Away

CAMPGROUNDS ⛰

Douglas Fir ♿

Franklin D. Roosevelt's Civilian Conservation Corp (CCC) built some of America's finest campgrounds, and Douglas Fir is no exception. Situated near the village of Glacier, the large sites offer more privacy than most campgrounds. There's a camp shelter for nature talks in summer and paved loops for the kids to bike. Open seasonally; reservations accepted; pets allowed on leashes.

Silver Fir ♿

This campground is an excellent base camp for hiking in the summer; after it shuts down for the winter, it's a nonmotorized Sno-Park. Silver Fir is another CCC-built campground with spacious sites, all with access to the North Fork of the Nooksack River. The wide gravel bar is a sunny place to plant yourself and enjoy the music of the river. Reservations available; pets allowed on leashes.

Horseshoe Cove ♿

This 39-site campground on Baker Lake offers more space and privacy than the larger campgrounds. It's a popular camp with a large swimming area, a broad beach, and a boat ramp. Reserve early! Pets allowed on leashes; closed in winter.

Bayview and Bayview North ♿ (partial)

These two adjacent campgrounds are situated on the shore of Baker Lake, with Bayview North having large group campsites available. All sites have a picnic table and fire ring. Pets allowed on leashes; reservations available; closed in winter.

Boulder Creek

A small, quiet campground on Boulder Creek, removed from the enthusiastic Baker Lake crowd. There are 9 sites: 5 reservable; 3 first come, first served; and 1 group. No potable water—bring your own or filter it from the creek. Pets allowed on leashes; closed in winter.

Panorama Point 🛆

Small with only 15 campsites and no potable water, Panorama Point sits on the Baker Lake shore with stellar views. Many day trippers come to use the boat ramp, especially during sockeye salmon season, and the picnic shelter has the best seat in the house. Reservations available; pets allowed on leashes; closed in winter.

Swift Creek 🛆

If you're a boater who loves to fish, this is the Baker Lake campground for you: a paved boat ramp, a 20-slip marina to tie up your boat (for a fee), a small beach, and potable water add to the amenities of fire rings and picnic tables. The 50-site campground is especially busy during the sockeye salmon run in July and August as anglers head out to test their luck on the lake. Reservable; pets allowed on leashes; closed in winter.

Shannon Creek 🛆

Near the end of Baker Lake, Shannon Creek is off the beaten track and one of the more mellow campgrounds of the Baker Lake area. It's small, with only 19 campsites (11 of which can be reserved), but it has a shady picnic area, a pebbly beach, and a boat ramp available only to Shannon Creek campground users. There's a gorgeous view of Mount Watson across the lake. No potable water; pets allowed on leashes; closed during the winter.

CABINS AND LODGES 🏠

The Mountaineers' Mount Baker Lodge

Near the Mount Baker ski area, this rustic lodge is run by the Seattle Mountaineers club and open to both members and nonmembers. The dorm-style sleeping accommodations are divided into men's, women's, and family areas with a communal lounge and dining hall. On weekends your stay includes Saturday and Sunday breakfast and a Saturday night dinner. Count on an enthusiastic 7:00 a.m. wake-up call to greet the day. Open year-round and surrounded by multiple outdoor adventure opportunities, the lodge is a cheerful alternative to camping. *mountaineers.org*

Snowater Resort ♿

Snowater manages the rentals of privately owned condominiums distributed over 27 acres of old-growth forest off the Mount Baker Scenic Highway. There are indoor pools with a hot tub and sauna, a fitness and workout room, and tennis and pickleball courts. No pets allowed.

LOOKOUTS

Park Butte Lookout

The moderately difficult 3.8 mile hike to this first-come, first-served lookout is spectacular with wildflower-laced meadows and staggering views of Mount Baker. If others are overnighting in the building, there are other campsites in the area. Summer weekends bring crowds and it's best to get there by 10:00 a.m. if you want to claim it. No charge to stay, but bring water and pack out all your waste. Keep in mind there is a seasonal bridge on the trail that is removed in the early fall and typically replaced in late spring. Park Butte Lookout is lovingly maintained by volunteers of the Skagit Alpine Club. For more on Pacific Northwest lookouts, see page 160. *fs.usda.gov*

Season of Green

DAY HIKES

1. Horseshoe Bend 😊 ⚘ ⚙ 🐾

- Northwest Forest Pass
- Easy
- 2.4 miles round trip out and back
- 220 feet elevation gain
- 1 hour

Get out the sketch pad and take your time to pause and paint and wander down this gentle and engaging trail. The trailhead is just across the road from Douglas Fir campground and eventually fades away after a mile or so. *wta.org*

2. Boyd Creek Interpretive Trail ☺ ⚲ ✿ 🐾 🚶

- **Northwest Forest Pass**
- **Easy**
- **0.5-mile loop**

- **No elevation gain**
- **30 minutes**

Most of this 0.5-mile trail is boardwalk, making it easy for small children and those with mobility issues. The focus is on salmon and steelhead and their habitat, and if you enjoy interpretive trails, this is a gem. *nps.gov/noca/learn /news/upload/Page6-7Mt.Baker%20RD.pdf*

3. Skyline Divide ⚲ ✿ 🌿 🐾 ✦

- **Northwest Forest Pass**
- **Moderate**
- **9 miles round trip out and back**

- **2,500 feet elevation gain**
- **5–6 hours**

Unrivaled mountain views from the top of the world and endless meadows filled with wildflowers will light your way on the Skyline Divide. After several ascending miles, the trail busts open to a ridgeline that gently rolls through a spectacular landscape. Slip a wildflower guide in your pack; the diversity is extraordinary. *wta.org*

4. Excelsior Peak via Damfino Lakes ⚲ ✿ 🌿 🐾 ✦

- **Northwest Forest Pass**
- **Moderate**
- **6.5 miles round trip out and back**

- **1,200 feet elevation gain**
- **4 hours**

Sometimes just the name of a hike is a draw and Damfino is one example, apparently named when someone asked a ranger what the small jeweled ponds were called. "Damn if I know," he replied, and so Excelsior Peak via Damfino was the route chosen. It's a glorious hike with knockout views and carpets of wildflowers in early August. When you reach Excelsior Pass, the meadowed ridge overlooking the Skagit Range demands a pause and a photo. Turn around and head back or check out the Skyline Divide for 0.5 mile. *wta.org*

5. Yellow Aster Butte ⚲ ⚙ 🌟 🐾

- **Northwest Forest Pass**
- **Difficult**
- **7.5 miles round trip out and back**
- **2,550 feet elevation gain**
- **4–5 hours**

When you ask locals for their favorite hikes, Yellow Aster is consistently on the list, and it's easy to see why. The wildflowers are stunning and you'll have front-row views of shimmering tarns, Mount Baker, and a beautiful complex of North Cascades peaks. It's a popular summer hike but the fall colors in September without the crowds are even better. You'll work for this one, but don't miss it. Keep in mind all alpine ecosystems are fragile; the plant life grows by the inch and is killed by the foot. Take care and stay on the trails. *wta.org*

6. Picture Lake ☺ ⚙ 🐾 🌟 ♿

- **Northwest Forest Pass**
- **Easy**
- **0.5-mile loop**
- **Negligible elevation gain**
- **30 minutes**

Picture Lake is a virtual postcard with the classic vista of Mount Shuksan reflected in its still water and framed in wildflowers. This trail is ADA-accessible and gives all people the opportunity to breathe in the beauty. Interpretive signs explain the geological history. *wta.org*

7. Fire and Ice ☺ ⚙ 🐾 🌟 ♿

- **Northwest Forest Pass**
- **Easy**
- **0.5-mile loop**
- **60 feet elevation gain**
- **30 minutes**

This is one of the first trails in the Heather Meadows area to melt out in spring. All trails from here have a wow factor for the unsurpassed setting and this one is no exception. Add accessibility by wheelchair and the opportunity to learn more about the volcanic history of the region, and you have a winning combination. *wta.org*

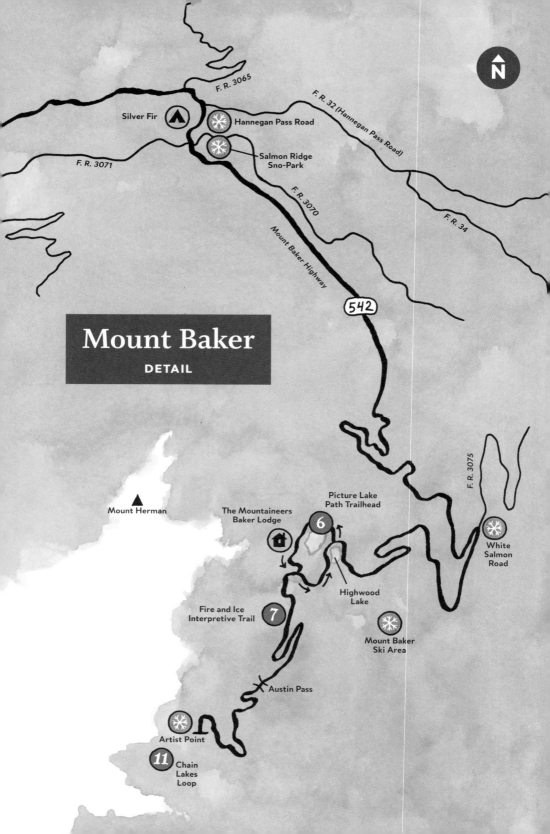

Mount Baker

DETAIL

N

F. R. 3065

Silver Fir

Hannegan Pass Road

F. R. 32 (Hannegan Pass Road)

Salmon Ridge
Sno-Park

F. R. 3071

F. R. 3070

F. R. 34

Mount Baker Highway

542

F. R. 3075

Mount Herman

The Mountaineers
Baker Lodge

Picture Lake
Path Trailhead

6

White
Salmon
Road

Highwood
Lake

Fire and Ice
Interpretive Trail

7

Mount Baker
Ski Area

Austin Pass

Artist Point

11 Chain
Lakes
Loop

8. Shadow of the Sentinels ☺ ⚱ 👣 ♿

- Northwest Forest Pass
- Easy
- 0.5-mile loop

- 50 feet elevation gain
- 30 minutes

Stop the car, stretch your legs, and check out big old trees along a sweet loop that is accessible for strollers and folks with mobility issues. *wta.org*

9. Baker Lake ☺ ⚱ ✿ 🍂 👣 ✦

- Northwest Forest Pass
- Easy
- 14 miles one way (park cars at both ends)

- 1,358 feet elevation gain
- 7 hours

This 14-mile hike from the south start of the Baker Lake trail to the Baker River trailhead can be hiked in all seasons when other trails are snowbound. It's a long and lovely walk through a forested canopy along and above the lake. Several side trails access beaches for shoreside picnics. Start at either end, or traverse the first 5 miles and return. *fs.usda.gov*

10. Baker River ☺ ⚱ ✿ 🍂 👣 ✦

- Northwest Forest Pass
- Easy
- 5 miles round trip out and back

- 300 feet elevation gain
- 2.5 hours

Listen to the music of the river along this trail and let nature's white noise quiet your thoughts and pull you into a corridor teeming with life. Baker River is born of melting glaciers and ice fields, and the trail meanders beside the current as you pass old-growth cedars rising straight and strong. Others are visually arresting with limbs and roots twisted around giant boulders. You don't want to miss this trail. *fs.usda.gov*

MULTIDAY BACKPACKING

11. Chain Lakes Loop ☺ ⚙ ✂ 🐾 ☀

- Northwest Forest Pass, wilderness permit self-issued at trailhead
- Moderate

- 6.5 miles round trip out and back
- 1,820 feet elevation gain
- 3 hours one way

This summer-only hike is one of the standout trails of Heather Meadows and it's teeming with people, particularly on weekends. Go midweek at the end of August if possible. You'll reap the rewards of subalpine lakes, flower-lit meadows, and views of formidable mountain peaks. There are two campsite options: 4 sites at Hayes Lake and 4 at Mazama Lakes. To help preserve this fragile ecosystem, you must camp at designated campsites only, marked with posts. *wta.org*

12. Park Butte ⚙ ✂ 🐾 ☀

- Northwest Forest Pass, wilderness permit self-issued at trailhead
- Moderate

- 8 miles round trip out and back
- 2,200 feet elevation gain
- 5–6 hours

Ending at Park Butte Lookout, this is one of the most stunning hikes in the Mount Baker region. It's a virtual Disneyland of alpine lakes, chattering creeks, wildflowers in wide meadows, and views of massive mountains that are pinch-me beautiful. There are even gifts in the dark when the Milky Way sweeps across the sky on clear nights. All this, and only a moderate-rated hike. Your campsite destination is Cathedral Camp, just off the main trail about 1 mile before the climb up to the lookout. Camping is allowed in designated sites only, and if Cathedral Rock is full there are several campsites along the Railroad Grade trail about 0.5 mile back down. Using Cathedral Camp as a base allows you to climb the approximate 1 mile to the lookout (for more on lookouts, see page 160) and snag it for the night if it's empty. You can also explore the nearby Railroad Grade (don't let the prosaic name fool you; it's a lovely hike), and Bell Pass. Pro tip: Everyone loves Park Butte. Be at the trailhead early with your poles and snow and ice footwear traction. Snowfields linger late into July. *wta.org*

13. Anderson Point or Maple Grove via Baker Lake Trail

😊 ⚙ 🐾 👣 ✨ ♨

- Northwest Forest
- Easy
- 4 to 8 miles round trip out and back

- 500 feet elevation gain
- 1–2 hours one way

Escape the crowds on the east side of Baker Lake for this glorious hike down the southern portion of the Baker Lake Trail. Anderson Point at 2 miles or Maple Grove at 4 miles is your camping destination; note that the trail continues along the lake for another 6.5 miles once past Maple Grove. What's not to love? With old-growth forest, waterfalls, a dip in the lake, frogs and birds, and little elevation gain, this backpacking trip is ideal for families and first timers. The trail is open year-round. *wta.org*

14. Anderson and Watson Lakes 😊 ⚙ 🌿 👣 ✨

- Northwest Forest Pass
- Easy to moderate
- 6 miles round trip out and back to Watson Lakes

- 1,600 feet elevation gain
- 3 hours

It's a rollercoaster trail with pitches of breathtaking beauty, especially if you remember to turn around and look at Mount Baker along the way. There are two options for camping: Anderson Lake—an easier, less crowded choice—and Watson Lakes. Both are fine subalpine jewels, and both are notoriously buggy before first frost. Plan a sunrise hike to Anderson Butte in the morning, 2 miles back down the trail from Watson Lake (1 mile from the trailhead), a demanding but worthy trek. *wta.org*

EXPLORE MORE ADVENTURES

Get Mist-Kissed by Nooksack Falls

Nooksack Falls is one of the most popular thunderous waterfalls in the North Cascades, resplendent with two segmented plunges crashing 88 feet down and cinematic enough to be the setting for a scene in the movie *The Deer Hunter*. The falls are a short walk from the parking lot, where a kiosk describes the history and the ongoing production of hydroelectricity from a power plant built in 1906. Take the danger signs around the falls seriously; several people have died over the years falling on slippery rocks while attempting an up-close photo. *waterfallsnorthwest.com*

Watch the Sunset at Artist Point

State Route 542 ends at Artist Point with 360-degree views of Mount Baker, Mount Shuksan, and the North Cascades. It is an arresting place of singular beauty available to all—from either the parking lot or a short walk to reflecting lakes and tarns. At 5,000 feet elevation, the road is open only for 3 months, typically from mid-July to late September. The rest of the year it's buried under the epic snowfalls of the region and then becomes a snowshoer's paradise.

Soak in Baker Hot Springs

This hot springs experience is a gamble: after miles of driving a rough potholed gravel road, you might have the forested pools to yourself, or you might encounter a horde of naked people drinking beer. Come early in the morning; the crowds tend to come later in the day. It's a 10-minute hike up to the three pools, and they are lovely. Heated by the region's volcanic activity, the main pool can comfortably fit seven people. Swimsuits optional, but expect nudity. *alltrails.com*

Kayak to a Campout: Baker Lake Paddle to Maple Grove or Anderson Point

Rent a sea kayak in Bellingham if you don't own one (it has waterproof hatches for your camp gear), and put in at one of the Baker Lake campgrounds with a boat ramp (Horseshoe Cove, for example, is less than a mile across the lake from Anderson Point camp; see link below and Hike #13: Anderson Point). You can pay to park your car there. This is an excellent kayak campout for first timers: the lake is long and skinny, which means you are reasonably close to shore the whole paddle. Camp on the east side at either Anderson Point, Maple Grove, or Noisy Creek. The campsites can be crowded with hikers in the summer, but if you plan your paddle midweek and leave early in the morning, you'll have a good chance of finding one. Even better are the shoulder seasons of spring and fall. After your paddle, set up camp and spend the day (or two or three) paddling the calm waters of the lake and hiking the Baker Lake Trail. *fs.usda.gov*

Season of Snow

Welcome to one of the most heavily snowed regions in North America, with an average of 53 feet of snow on the mountain each winter. Because of the heavy snowfall it is critical to be aware of avalanche danger during all your winter activities in the Mount Baker area. Always check the avalanche forecast, the weather forecast, and the road conditions before you go. *nwac.us*

SNOWSHOE TRAILS

Ranger-Guided Walk

For a small donation you can learn about the terrain and the ecology of the Mount Baker area with an experienced guide from the US Forest Service. Snowshoes and poles are provided. *fs.usda.gov*

White Salmon Road

A great trail for families and beginners, this route gently descends 2.5 miles; then you'll have to snowshoe back up to the car. You'll enjoy knockout views of Mount Shuksan and the Upper Nooksack Valley on clear days, with no avalanche danger. *wta.org*

Salmon Ridge Sno-Park

This groomed cross-country ski area maintained by Washington State Parks has several designated meandering trails for snowshoers (no snowshoeing allowed on cross-country trails), including White Salmon Creek, an easy family-friendly trail. Sno-Park permit required. *wta.org*

Hannegan Pass Road

One of the easiest and most accessible snow trails in the Nooksack River valley, the trail climbs gently for the first mile with Mount Shuksan claiming the skyline on clear days. Then the trail steepens for several miles. There is significant avalanche danger after 3 miles, so return at that point. *mountaineers.org*

Artist Point

Artist Point has one of the most spectacular vistas in the entire state, and the 2-mile snowshoe from the ski area up to the point is stunning if you don't mind working for it. Go midweek on a clear day if possible; the trail is often crowded on weekends. *wta.org*

CROSS-COUNTRY SKI TRAILS

Nooksack Nordic Ski Club

While there is no Nordic center at Mount Baker, the Nooksack Nordic Ski Club is the hub for all cross-country ski trail information in the area. From overnight ski trips to grooming reports to a complete list of trails in the area, their website is a jewel that will guide you through the changeable winter conditions and avalanche danger levels of the Mount Baker region. *nooksacknordicskiclub.org*

DOWNHILL SKI AND SNOWBOARD TRIPS

Mount Baker Ski Area

Mount Baker is off the beaten track, a true local's mountain with a great deal to offer both skiers and boarders. The stats: 8 lifts, 2 rope tows, and 1,000 skiable acres. Unlike at other Pacific Northwest ski resorts, you won't have lift-line waits or worry about snow coverage. Self-contained campers and RVs are allowed to park overnight in designated areas. Mount Baker is also home to the Legendary Banked Slalom, a slalom snowboard race through a natural half-pipe; it's held in February each winter. There's no prize money—the winner receives a duct tape trophy and a logoed Carhartt jacket. *mtbaker.us*

SLEDDING AND TUBING

Sledding Free-For-All

There's always snow at Mount Baker in winter, so when the snow is scant in urban centers, this is the place to be. There is no formal sledding site with tube rentals and helmets and signed releases; instead, take an independent,

MOUNT SHUKSAN, WASHINGTON

fun-filled romp around Picture Lake and on the slopes near the parking lot where State Route 542 is gated in winter. There's no sledding allowed in the ski area.

EXPLORE MORE ADVENTURES

Watch Eagles Fly and Feed

From late November through January, thousands of bald eagles arrive along the shores of the North Fork of the Nooksack River to plunder the decomposing bodies of spawned-out chum salmon. It's an astounding scene in the salmon life cycle; they make a massive contribution to the ecosystem of the Pacific Northwest. The best place to watch is 1 mile off State Route 542 at Deming Homestead Eagle Park.

Snow Camp at Artist Point

The 2-mile snowshoe to Artist Point is a thing of beauty in itself, but add an overnight and you have an adventure to remember. Watch the weather—time it for a clear night—and you'll have sweeping views of Mount Baker and the Cascade Range. Snowshoe in from the trailhead in the upper lot at Mount Baker Ski Area. At camp, the alpenglow of sunset washes over the landscape before the stars take center stage. The trail passes through avalanche terrain, so always check the avalanche forecast before you go.

HAWKS AND EAGLES

GOLDEN EAGLE

BALD EAGLE

OSPREY

COOPER'S HAWK

RED-TAILED HAWK

NORTHERN HARRIER

PEREGRINE FALCON

MERLIN

AMERICAN KESTREL

AMERICAN KESTREL

OSPREY

PEREGRINE FALCON

MERLIN

BALD EAGLE

GOLDEN EAGLE

COOPER'S HAWK

RED-TAILED HAWK

NORTHERN HARRIER

ALPINE LAKES WILDERNESS AREA, WASHINGTON

Central Cascades, Washington

Stevens Pass, Alpine Lakes Wilderness, Snoqualmie Region

Washington's Central Cascades are a mecca of year-round mountain adventures less than 2 hours by car from Seattle. The focus of this chapter is on the Stevens Pass region, the Interstate 90 corridor (including Snoqualmie and Cle Elum), and the Alpine Lakes Wilderness area (Leavenworth). The Alpine Lakes Wilderness area alone sprawls for over 400,000 acres and is studded with more than 700 lakes and tarns that give the wilderness its name. These alpine lakes are exquisitely clear from the icy-cold water, which inhibits algae growth, and they're commonly set in glacier-scooped basins ringed by formidable peaks. The Alpine Lakes Wilderness contains some of the most ruggedly magnificent topography in the Cascade Range.

Get Away

CAMPGROUNDS ⋀

Beckler River (Stevens Pass) ⅋

Here there are spacious reservable campsites along the Beckler River with a few sites along the shore. It's close to a wide variety of recreation activities, including Stevens Pass ski area, a 20-minute drive away. Pets allowed on leashes.

Eightmile (Alpine Lakes Wilderness/Leavenworth) ⅋

Located 8 miles down Icicle Creek Road, this large and pleasant campground has 41 well-spaced sites, 4 double-family sites, and a reservable group site; 60 percent of the sites are reservable and 40 percent are first come, first served. Pets allowed on leashes; closed in winter.

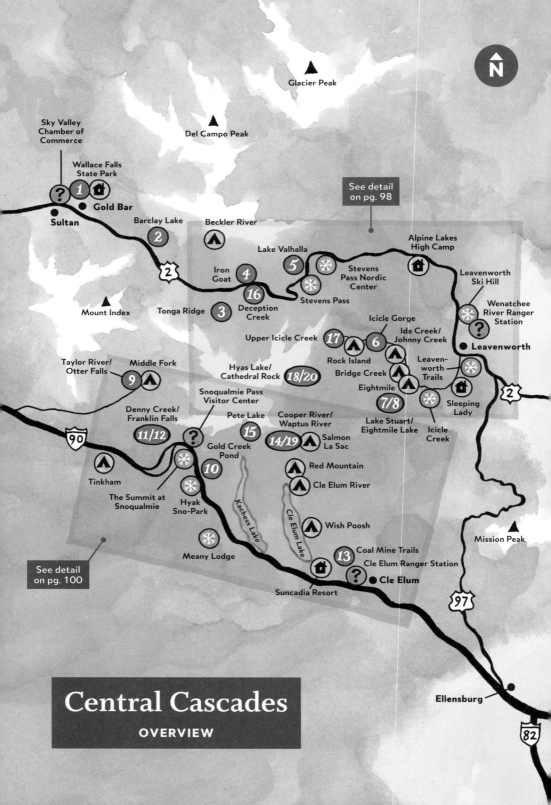

Central Cascades

OVERVIEW

N

Glacier Peak

Del Campo Peak

Sky Valley Chamber of Commerce

Wallace Falls State Park

? 1 🏠

● Gold Bar

Sultan

Barclay Lake

2

Beckler River

🏕

Iron Goat

4

16

Tonga Ridge

3

Deception Creek

Mount Index

Lake Valhalla

5

❄

❄

Stevens Pass Nordic Center

Stevens Pass

See detail on pg. 98

Alpine Lakes High Camp

🏠

Leavenworth Ski Hill

Wenatchee River Ranger Station

❄

?

● Leavenworth

Icicle Gorge

Upper Icicle Creek

17

🏕

6

Ida Creek/ Johnny Creek

🏕

Rock Island

Bridge Creek

🏕

Leaven- worth Trails

❄

Hyas Lake/ Cathedral Rock

18/20

🏠

Eightmile

7/8

❄

Sleeping Lady

Taylor River/ Otter Falls

9 🏕

Middle Fork

Lake Stuart/ Eightmile Lake

Icicle Creek

2

Denny Creek/ Franklin Falls

11/12

Snoqualmie Pass Visitor Center

?

Pete Lake

15

Gold Creek Pond

Cooper River/ Waptus River

14/19

Salmon La Sac

90

❄

10

❄

Red Mountain

🏕

🏕 Tinkham

Hyak Sno-Park

❄

Cle Elum River

Kachess Lake

Cle Elum Lake

🏕 Wish Poosh

Mission Peak

The Summit at Snoqualmie

Meany Lodge

❄

13

Coal Mine Trails

Cle Elum Ranger Station

🏠

?

● Cle Elum

See detail on pg. 100

Suncadia Resort

97

Ellensburg ●

82

Bridge Creek (Alpine Lakes Wilderness/Leavenworth)

This small campground is a gem on the confluence of Bridge and Icicle Creeks. It has 6 first-come, first-served sites, but it's used more for its spacious reservable group site that holds up to 75 people. It's a popular spot for groups of rock climbers to meet up and camp for easy access to nearby crags. Pets allowed on leashes; closed in winter.

Johnny Creek (Alpine Lakes Wilderness/Leavenworth) ♿

Another first-come, first-served campground, it's one of the largest on Icicle Creek Road, with 65 sites divided into upper and lower campgrounds. The upper campsites are more wooded. Both campgrounds fill quickly—arrive in the morning or preferably midweek to beat the crowds. Pets allowed on leashes; closed in winter.

Rock Island (Alpine Lakes Wilderness/Leavenworth) ♿

Icicle Creek widens and slows into pools here, making a divine backdrop for your camp experience. There are 22 well-spaced sites, and side trails lead down to the creek for swimming. Bonus: it's another first-come, first-served campground. In the summer arrive in the morning, or midweek if possible, for a better chance at snagging a site. Pets allowed on leashes; closed in winter.

Ida Creek (Alpine Lakes Wilderness/Leavenworth) ♿

These 10 large first-come, first-served sites are on the confluence of Ida and Icicle Creeks, a picturesque setting farther off Icicle Creek Road than other campgrounds for a quieter stay, with swimming holes adding to its charm. Vault toilets; ADA accessible; pets allowed on leashes; closed in winter.

Tinkham (Snoqualmie) ♿

At this family-friendly campground, the Tinkham Discovery Trail leads to a sweet pond. With its proximity to I-90 you'll hear traffic, but you're also close to numerous trailheads. The 47 sites are a mix of reservable and first come, first served. Pets allowed on leashes; closed in winter.

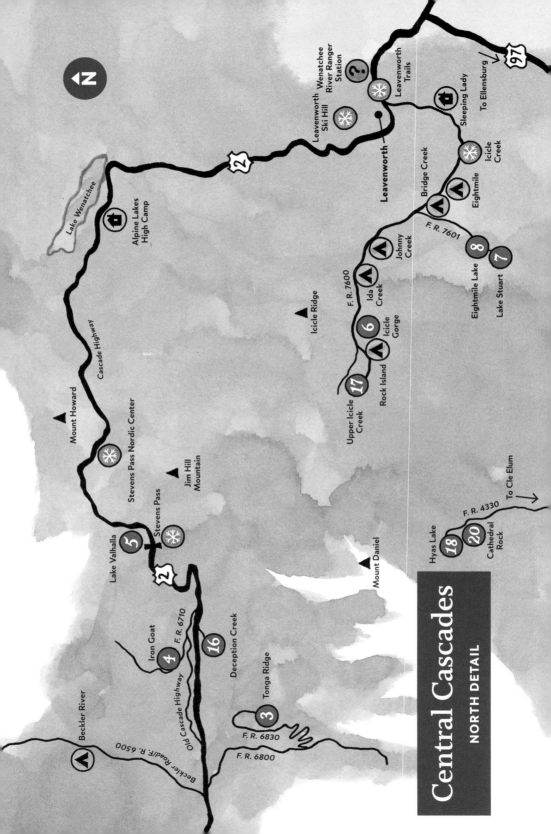

Central Cascades
NORTH DETAIL

Middle Fork (Snoqualmie) ♿

Get away from the din of I-90 traffic at this secluded campground on the North Fork of the Snoqualmie River. There are ample sites to hold large groups and, on a clear day, stunning views of Mount Baker. The easy access to multiple hiking trails and the river music of the North Fork lulling you to sleep at night make this a great campground. There are 39 reservable sites. Pets allowed on leashes; closed in winter.

Wish Poosh (Cle Elum) ♿

The name comes from a Chinook creation story involving the angry Great Beaver Wishpoosh, who carved lakes with his thrashing tail. The campground has a beautiful setting on the southeastern shore of Cle Elum Lake, with the wide, sandy Speelyi Beach nearby. There are 34 reservable campsites for both tents and RVs. On weekends there's a 2-night minimum stay; on holidays, 3 nights. Pets allowed on leashes; closed in winter.

Cle Elum River (Cle Elum)

This lovely campground has 23 individual sites (14 first come, first served) and a reservable group site with a capacity for 100 people. Situated at the head of Cle Elum Lake, along the Cle Elum River and with Speelyi Beach nearby, it's a great location for your adventure base camp. Pets allowed on leashes; closed in winter.

Red Mountain (Cle Elum) ♿

Small, primitive, and with a great swimming hole on the Cle Elum River, this first-come, first-served campground is off the beaten track; 8 of the 10 sites are on the river. Pets allowed on leashes; closed in winter.

Salmon La Sac (Cle Elum)

This expansive campground has 69 sites for both tents and RVs, 40 of them reservable. Salmon La Sac is popular with anglers, hikers, and mountain bikers for the abundance of nearby recreation opportunities. It's closed seasonally, but 0.5 mile south is a Sno-Park with access to groomed ski trails through the campground. Pets allowed on leashes.

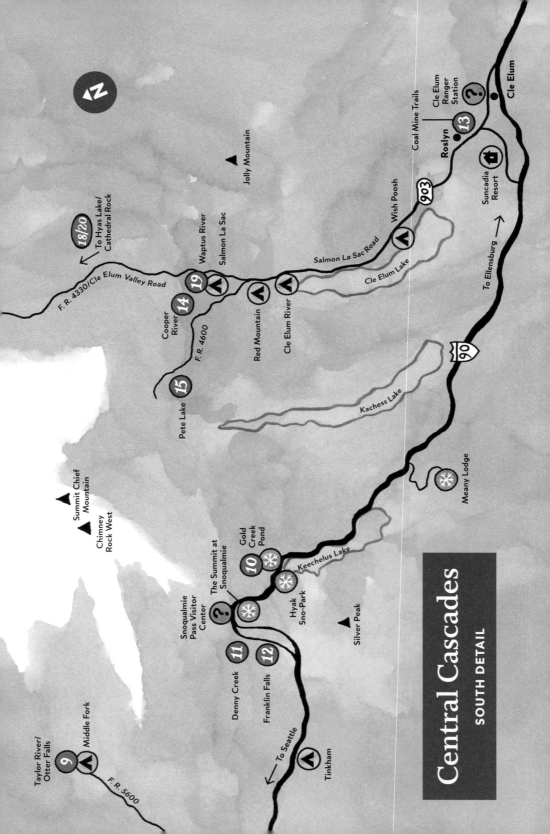

Central Cascades

SOUTH DETAIL

N

To Hyas Lake/
Cathedral Rock
18/20

F. R. 4330/Cle Elum Valley Road

Jolly Mountain

Waptus River
Salmon La Sac

19

Cooper
River
14

Red Mountain

Cle Elum River

F. R. 4600

15

Pete Lake

Salmon La Sac Road

Cle Elum Lake

Wish Poosh

903

Coal Mine Trails

Cle Elum
Ranger
Station
?

13

Roslyn

Cle Elum

Suncadia Resort

To Ellensburg

90

Kachess Lake

Summit Chief
Mountain

Chimney
Rock West

Meany Lodge

Gold
Creek
Pond

10

Keechelus Lake

Snoqualmie
Pass Visitor
Center
?

The Summit at
Snoqualmie

Hyak
Sno-Park

Silver Peak

11

Denny Creek

12

Franklin Falls

To Seattle

Tinkham

Taylor River/
Otter Falls

Middle Fork

9

F. R. 5600

CABINS AND LODGES 🏠

Wallace Falls State Park Cabins (Stevens Pass) ♿

Base yourself at one of these rustic cabins for year-round adventure: access to 12 miles of hiking trails threading through old-growth forest to lakes and waterfalls, and in the winter, snowshoeing right out the back door. Each cabin sleeps up to five people on bunks and a futon; there's electricity and heat but no kitchen, and you'll need to bring your own bedding or sleeping bag. Side note: there are also 2 very private first-come, first-served campsites at the park. Open year-round.

Alpine Lakes High Camp (Stevens Pass)

This unique camp offers 9 backcountry cabins on private gated land, where trailheads lead deep into the Alpine Lakes Wilderness for summer hiking and great backcountry and cross-country skiing in the winter. The staff will shuttle you and your gear up a long winding road from a parking lot off Highway 2. Although the cabins have no electricity or water, there is a common kitchen in the small lodge and a wood-fired hot tub and sauna on-site. Open year-round.

Sleeping Lady (Alpine Lakes Wilderness/Leavenworth) ♿

Sleeping Lady is tucked away on the banks of Icicle Creek near Leavenworth, with gourmet cuisine, cozy accommodations, an outdoor terrace, and plenty of outdoor adventures within minutes of the resort. Hike, bike, river raft, and rock climb the day away, and then return here to sit back, enjoy the view while sipping a brew, sleep well, and do it all again the next day.

Suncadia (Snoqualmie) ♿

It would be easy to pigeonhole Suncadia as just another Disneyesque resort, but it's more than that, not only for adults on a romantic weekend away but for families who enjoy the outdoors. The resort is a vacation community in the Cascade foothills set on over 6,000 acres, with hiking trails, paddling, fishing, swimming pools for the kids, and in winter, an outdoor ice-skating rink and sledding hills. There are rooms in a swanky lodge and freestanding houses to rent, a farm-to-table restaurant, and a spa to pamper yourself post-hike.

Season of Green

For all hikes in this section, check *wta.org* for directions and the latest beta information.

DAY HIKES

1. Wallace Falls (Stevens Pass) ⚲ 🐾 ⭐ ♨

- Discover Pass
- Easy to moderate
- 5.5 miles round trip out and back
- 1,300 feet elevation gain
- 3–4 hours

On this all-season trail with not one but nine waterfalls, Wallace Falls is the star of the show: its dramatic tiered plunges drop 265 feet. It is one of the state's most popular attractions, in part because the hike there is gorgeous. Get to the trailhead early for the best experience. Pets are allowed, but the leash law is strictly enforced—a number of dogs have died going over the falls.

2. Barclay Lake (Stevens Pass) ☺ ⚙ 🐾

- Northwest Forest Pass
- Easy
- 4.4 miles round trip out and back
- 225 feet elevation gain
- 2.5 hours

This gentle hike follows Barclay Creek most of the way to the lake, and thanks to the heavy precipitation of the area, it can be foot-stompingly muddy and great fun for kids. The lake is snuggled up against Merchant Peak and the looming Baring Mountain. With established backcountry campsites and picnic spots around its shore, it's also a great beginner's overnight backpack.

3. Tonga Ridge (Stevens Pass) ☺ ⚙ ✄ 🐾

- Northwest Forest Pass
- 400 feet elevation gain
- Easy
- 3 hours
- 6 miles round trip out and back

Tonga Ridge is a huckleberry hike if ever there was one. Autumn is prime time for this rolling ridge trail that skirts just inside the Alpine Lakes Wilderness. From the trail take a 1-mile northerly detour to summit Mount Sawyer, the site of an old fire lookout, for powerful views of Mount Daniel and Mount Hinman. Return to the main trail and carry on to Sawyer Pass in another mile, then turn around and head back.

4. Iron Goat Trail Loop (Stevens Pass) ☠ ⚙ 🐾 ♨ 🦌

- Northwest Forest Pass
- 700 feet elevation gain
- Easy to moderate
- 3 hours
- 6-mile loop

This trail is a beautiful combination of history and hiking, enhanced if you read Gary Krist's enthralling book on the heartbreaking 1910 disaster that took place along it, *The White Cascade: The Great Northern Railway Disaster and America's Deadliest Avalanche*. The tunnels and snowsheds, as well as interpretive signs, tell the rail story along a gentle forested trail. The first 3 miles are ADA accessible.

5. Lake Valhalla (Stevens Pass) ☺ ⚙ ✄ 🐾 ✶ ♨

- Northwest Forest Pass*
- 1,500 feet elevation gain
- Easy to moderate
- 3.5–4 hours
- 7 miles round trip out and back

Bring your sketchbook to record this sweet trail through meadows, the sandy beach at the lake, and Lichtenberg Mountain in postcard granite glory. Come midweek to avoid weekend crowds. For a backpacking option, stay the night on the shores of Lake Valhalla; there are crowds during the summer months, but who can blame them?

If you are accessing the trail from the Stevens Pass parking lot, you don't need a pass.

6. Icicle Gorge Nature Loop (Alpine Lakes Wilderness/Leavenworth)

- Northwest Forest Pass
- Easy
- 4 miles
- 150 feet elevation gain
- 1.5–2 hours

I can't think of a better way to end the hours spent in a car than hiking this gentle interpretive trail. The Icicle River running through the gorge, however, is anything but gentle. It seethes and swerves and hurtles between the narrow granite walls, filling the air with thunder while you watch from a broad trail beside it. This hike is ideal for families, beginner hikers, trail runners, bird-watchers, and anyone who enjoys learning more about this stunning corner of the Pacific Northwest.

7. Lake Stuart (Alpine Lakes Wilderness/Leavenworth)

- Northwest Forest Pass, wilderness permit self-issued at trailhead
- Moderate
- 10 miles round trip out and back
- 1,680 feet elevation gain
- 5–6 hours

Lake Stuart is the beautiful, smaller sister of nearby Colchuck Lake, off the beaten trail and often overlooked. You'll encounter far fewer people and enjoy a gentler trail through a parallel valley that follows Mountaineer Creek, with an impressive view of Argonaut Peak along the way. Bonus: Lake Stuart is shallower and warmer than other alpine lakes in the region, inviting you in for a dip in late summer.

8. Eightmile Lake (Alpine Lakes Wilderness/Leavenworth)

- Northwest Forest Pass, wilderness permit self-issued at trailhead
- Moderate
- 7.8 miles round trip out and back
- 1,400 feet elevation gain
- 4–5 hours

Along the first half of the trail there are burnt swathes from a fire in 2012, but at the feet of the ghostly trees is a living testament to the regeneration after a scorching burn: the profuse waves of wildflowers, the abundance and variety of birds, and the stretch of tree seedlings reaching for the sky. You'll also take in chattering streams, formidable peaks, and the stately grace of live ponderosa pines as you hike to this large and lovely lake.

9. Taylor River/Otter Falls (Snoqualmie) ☺ ⚲ 🦋 🐾 〰

- Northwest Forest Pass
- Easy to moderate
- 11 miles round trip out and back
- 650 feet elevation gain
- 6 hours

Less than an hour from Seattle you can wander down through an old-growth forest into tranquil wilderness and encounter magnificent Otter Falls, a sliding horsetail falls that drops 1,200 feet into tiny Lipsy Lake and into the Taylor River. The final climb to the falls is steep but short. The falls dry up in summer; spring is best for an abundant flow, but bring poles for balance while crossing the many small creeks and drainages you'll encounter on the trail.

10. Gold Creek Pond Loop (Snoqualmie) ☺ ⚙ 🦋 🐾 ♿

- Northwest Forest Pass; Sno-Park permit in winter
- Easy
- 1-mile loop
- 10 feet elevation gain
- 45 minutes

This gentle, paved hike is accessible to all—by stroller, wheelchair, or two tiny feet. Listen to the birds and watch the wildlife. It's amazing to think that in the 1970s and early '80s this was a gravel pit used in the construction of I-90; today it's a wonderful example of government agencies working together to restore and reclaim the landscape. It's more lake than pond, with plenty of access points to splash about and picnic tables and grills to settle at for the day.

11. Denny Creek (Snoqualmie) ☺ ⚲ ⚙ 🐾 〰

- Northwest Forest Pass
- Easy
- 2 miles round trip out and back
- 400 feet elevation gain
- 1 hour

Who can resist a forested hike to a natural granite waterslide on a hot summer day? Not many, it seems. Denny Creek is a popular escape from city heat and great fun for young and old. Ford the creek carefully at the slide (low water in summer is safest) and carry on for another 0.7 mile to the impressive Keekwulee Falls. There's an outcropping of rocks just off the trail for a picnic with a view.

12. Franklin Falls (Snoqualmie) ☺ ♀ 👪 ♨

- **Northwest Forest Pass**
- **Easy**
- **2 miles round trip out and back**
- **400 feet elevation gain**
- **1–1.5 hours**

Franklin Falls is a perfect family hike even for the three-year-olds among us (go at their pace!), with a stunning climax of a thundering three-tiered waterfall. You'll be able to see only the third tier, a sheer plunge into a pool, but it is impressive indeed, particularly during the peak of snowmelt in June and July. During those months prepare for mist kisses and watch your footing on the rocks. This is a wonderful hike year-round: in winter the falls often ice up spectacularly and the trail is an easy snowshoe.

13. Coal Mine Trails (Snoqualmie) ☺ ⚙ 🦅 👪

- **No pass required**
- **Easy**
- **9.5 miles round trip out and back**
- **450 feet elevation gain**
- **5 hours**

This trail is another lovely stroll through history, this time through the rich coal mining story of the region, with interpretive signs along the way. The wide and mellow trail from Cle Elum to Ronald was a railroad line until it was converted to a public recreation trail in 1994. Popular with bikers as well as hikers in summer, it's used in winter by snowshoers, cross-country skiers, and snowmobilers. Along the way stop in at charming Roslyn for lunch at the Roslyn Cafe, which was used as a set for the quirky TV series *Northern Exposure*.

14. Cooper River (Snoqualmie) ☺ ♀ ⚙ 🎣 🦅 👪 ♨

- **Northwest Forest Pass**
- **Easy to moderate**
- **8 miles round trip out and back**
- **400 feet elevation gain**
- **4 hours**

Hike this pleasing trail in the fall and you may see bright-red spawning sockeye salmon pooling at the base of Cooper Falls at the beginning of the hike. In 2009 the Yakama Nation reintroduced sockeye salmon here after 100 years of water development, mainly in the form of dams and diversions, that decimated the salmon population. Today you can see firsthand the beginning regeneration of fish that gave Salmon La Sac its name. The hike is family friendly, easy on the knees for older folks, and follows the Cooper River for much of its length. Pause at one of the flat riverside boulders, put your bare feet in the cold clear water, and contemplate the epic journey of salmon.

15. Pete Lake (Snoqualmie) ☺ ⚲ ✿ ⚶ ❦ 🐾

- Northwest Forest Pass
- Easy
- 9 miles round trip out and back
- 400 feet elevation gain
- 4 hours

Flee to the east side of the Cascades, where the sun shines when it's raining in Seattle, and head to Pete Lake: a jewel guarded by imposing granite mountains, with great campsites and a flat beach accessing the lake. This hike also makes a fabulous first overnight for little backpackers. Bring bug spray in the summer months; mosquitoes love this lake too.

MULTIDAY BACKPACKING

16. Deception Creek (Stevens Pass) ✿ ⚶ ♨ 🐾

- No pass required
- Moderate
- 8 miles round trip out and back
- 1,200 feet elevation gain
- 4.5 hours

This is a classic creek hike with waterfalls, swimming holes, campsites, and a trail tread that is broad and easy to navigate. The dripping moss is iridescent, the mushrooms worth a photograph, and the swathes of trillium in the spring will make you feel like Alice in Wonderland. At around 3 miles you'll come to a handful of campsites beside Deception Creek. Make your base here, and in the morning hike 0.5 mile farther up the trail to Deception Falls, or carry on to explore the Tonga Ridge trail or Deception Lakes.

TANK LAKE, ALPINE LAKES WILDERNESS AREA

17. Upper Icicle Creek (Alpine Lakes Wilderness/Leavenworth)
☺ 🦅 🐾

- Northwest Forest Pass
- Easy
- 3 miles round trip out and back

- 400 feet elevation gain
- 2 hours

An inviting hike to walk while talking with companions, this trail is level, green with trees and lush undergrowth, and a refreshing change from the more crowded hikes farther down Icicle Creek. At the confluence of Icicle and French Creeks, there are excellent campsites for families and backpacking first timers, and at night the soothing song of moving water is your background score. Set up camp here and the next day explore farther up the trail. Bring bug spray and mosquito nets to fit over your hat in the summer.

18. Hyas Lake (Snoqualmie) ☺ ⚙ ✂ 🦅 🐾

- Northwest Forest Pass
- Easy
- 4 miles round trip out and back

- 100 feet elevation gain
- 2 hours

Here's another east-of-the-rain-into-the-sun hike that is a wonderful backpacking trip to a lake you can swim and fish in. There are plenty of campsites and places to picnic along the shore, with several of the sites spacious enough for large groups. Con: the road to the trailhead is long and rough.

19. Waptus River to Waptus Lake (Snoqualmie) ⚙ ✂ 🦅 🐾

- Northwest Forest Pass
- Easy to moderate
- 18.8 miles round trip out and back

- 900 feet elevation gain
- 9.5–10 hours

This undulating trail winds through forests and then follows the Waptus River to Waptus Lake. There are multiple campsites along the way, and the lake—one of the largest in the Alpine Lakes Wilderness—offers even more sites. At 7.8 miles, you'll have to ford the river. A bridge washed out here in 2006 and hikers need to use the well-marked horse ford to cross. Plan this hike in the low water season of late summer or early autumn. Bring river shoes (or thick wool socks over your shoes or bare feet work in a pinch) and poles for balance. The end destination is worth the ford! You may even get the island campsite found just before the trail meets the Pacific Crest Trail at Spade Creek.

20. Cathedral Rock (Snoqualmie) ✿ ⚶ 🦋 🐾 ☀

- Northwest Forest Pass
- Moderate to difficult
- 8 miles round trip out and back
- 2,290 feet elevation gain
- 5 hours

Some hikes are worth the sweat and grind to get there, and this is one. You'll navigate the relentless switchbacks up to Squaw Lake (considered a derogatory term; there's a plan to change the name), draw a breath, and push on to Cathedral Rock, a landmark mountain that rises fiercely from the ridge. There are many pleasant campsites at Squaw Lake and you may want to set up your tent here, but the goal is a large unnamed tarn near Cathedral Pass, just before the Pacific Crest Trail junction, where there are established campsites for sitting back and considering the monolith and meadows.

EXPLORE MORE ADVENTURES

Mountain Bike at Stevens Pass

Stevens Pass has Washington State's only lift-served downhill bike park, with 10 trails ranging from easy to double black diamond. New to mountain biking? Take a lesson or attend a camp on-site to learn more about this exhilarating sport, then load the bike on the chairlift and enjoy the downhill cycle. Rental bikes available.

Learn to Rock Climb in Leavenworth

Maybe you've only practiced on a wall in a gym, or you're new to rock climbing, or you want to know the best climbs in the area: the highly rated Northwest Mountain School offers guided classes or one-on-one tutorials for all skill levels. All equipment provided. *mountainschool.com*

Tenkara Fly-Fish the Snoqualmie River

Tenkara is a Japanese form of fly-fishing that means "fishing from heaven." It's simple, using a long telescopic rod, a fixed line, and no reel. When you were a kid, did you tie a line to a stick to make a fishing pole? Tenkara is like that. Pure zen. All process. You typically use one fly for every creek and river, for all seasons. It's inexpensive, lightweight and packable, and very easy to learn. Whether you're an experienced angler or eager to learn the sport, tenkara will bring you into the wet heart of a mountain river or stream, and the romance of fly-fishing is yours.

River Raft the Wenatchee River

Spend a few hours on a lazy float, a white-knuckled paddle, or something in between: the Wenatchee River offers it all. The early-summer snow runoff brings wilder rides; later in the summer the water level drops and the river stretches idly with fewer rapids. Picnic, play in the water, ride those waves! There are many rafting companies in the area to choose from.

Hike into Goldmyer Hot Springs

This hot spring is a treasure snuggled into the foothills of the Cascades. Located at the end of a pleasant 4.5-mile hike, the hot springs are pristine and beautiful. It doesn't get much better than a geothermal soak in a lush mountain setting beside a waterfall. Goldmyer offers a sublime experience to those who make reservations (up to 1 month in advance only), and this is strictly enforced; all drop-ins are turned away. Expand the adventure: campsites on the grounds are available with a separate reservation and a fee.

Owl Prowl the Leavenworth Bird Fest

The Audubon Society rates Leavenworth as one of the best birding hot spots in Washington, and on the third weekend in May the Bird Fest celebrates migratory birds on their way north as well as the wide variety of resident birds. Events at this 4-day festival include daily birding excursions by raft, kayak, paddleboard, and bike, and yes, an owl prowl each night to encounter these shy and guarded birds. *wenatcheeriverinstitute.org*

Cycle the Iron Horse Tunnel

It's short, a bit scary, and disorienting, but there are few adventures like this 2-mile cycle down a completely dark old train tunnel. The trail is part of the 285-mile Palouse to Cascades Trail (formerly the John Wayne Pioneer Trail) that crosses Washington State, and you can pick it up on either side of the tunnel to lengthen your trip. Confirm that your bike light works, and bring a headlamp, extra batteries, and an extra jacket, preferably with reflective strips. The tunnel is damp as well as dark. Closed between November 1 and May 1. *wta.org*

Season of Snow

The Sno-Parks on the I-90 corridor offer miles of groomed trails for cross-country skiing and snowshoeing bliss. All snowshoers must stay to the side of groomed trails to save the smooth tracks from snowshoe prints. You'll need a Sno-Park pass and, for Sno-Parks with groomed trails, a special groomed trails permit (see link below for maps). The permits can be purchased online from November 1 to April 30. *Always* check the avalanche forecast! If you need a reason why, check out the incident reports via the Northwest Avalanche Center link below.

· For Sno-Park permits: *epermits.parks.wa.gov*
· For the Pacific Northwest avalanche forecast: *nwac.us*
· For Sno-Park trail maps that include groomed cross-country ski trails: *parks.state.wa.us*

SNOWSHOE TRAILS

Guided Snowshoe Trips

From January through March, the US Forest Service offers guided snowshoe tours at Stevens and Snoqualmie Passes to explore the winter ecology of the Central Cascades. For a small donation equipment is provided for the 90-minute and half-day hikes. Reservations required; make them January through February by calling Stevens Pass (360-677-2414) or Snoqualmie Pass (425-434-6111).

Lake Easton State Park also has guided snowshoe hikes on moderate terrain that last approximately 2.5 hours. Learn snowshoe techniques, the natural history of the area, and safety information. Bring your own snowshoes. To make reservations and for more information, call 509-925-1943. *waparks.org*

Gold Creek Pond (Snoqualmie)

This is an excellent place to practice beginning snowshoe skills—it's short (1 mile), flat, and well marked. It's popular with cross-country skiers as well and can be crowded on weekends. Sno-Park permit required. *wta.org*

Keechelus Lake (Snoqualmie)

From the Hyak Sno-Park, head south on the trail that leads to the lake. A former railroad grade, it's level and groomed (stay to the side to keep the cross-country tracks smooth), with lovely views of the lake and ridges. Turn around at the base of an avalanche chute at 2 miles. Sno-Park permit required. *mountaineers.org*

Icicle River Road (Alpine Lakes Wilderness/Leavenworth)

The upper portion of Icicle River Road is unplowed and gorgeous for snowshoeing and cross-country skiing, with imposing Cascade peaks on one side and a tumbling river on the other. The gradually ascending road ends 10 miles from Bridge Creek Campground. Go as far as you like, then return. *wta.org*

CROSS-COUNTRY SKI TRAILS

Stevens Pass Nordic Center

The Nordic Center has a variety of trails for novice to expert skiers. New to cross-country skiing? They also offer a first-timers package to help you master the basics with certified instructors. Day pass and rental equipment are included.

Leavenworth Winter Sports Club

The club maintains 26 miles of trails around Leavenworth with a variety of terrain to accommodate all skill levels, including the dog-friendly Waterfront Park trail. The club also offers 3 miles of lighted Nordic skiing at Leavenworth Ski Hill for cross-country night skiing.

DOWNHILL SKI AND SNOWBOARD TRIPS

The Summit at Snoqualmie

"This is where Seattle learns to ski and snowboard," the website proudly proclaims, and it's true. It's only an hour's drive from the city, there's plenty of parking, and there's a huge variety of terrain to play and ski in for all levels and interests, from sledding and snowshoeing to downhill skiing and snowboarding. There's something for everyone at the Summit's four base areas—Alpental, Summit West, Summit Central, and Summit East—with nearly 2,000 skiable acres.

Meany Lodge (Snoqualmie)

Built in 1928, Meany Lodge is one of the oldest ski areas in the United States that you've never heard of. The rustic lodge is just off exit 62 on I-90 and maintained by volunteers from the Mountaineers. There's a good selection of events in summer and fall—the mushroom foraging clinic is always a sellout—and the certified ski school, offering lessons in alpine skiing, snowboarding, snowshoeing, and cross-country skiing, is top-notch. Slopes are accessed with three rope tows. Reservations are required for both day use and overnight visits (all meals included; dormitory-style sleeping arrangements). You'll be towed up to the lodge by rope behind a snowcat, and you'll help clean up before you leave on Sunday. If you're looking for a respite from commercial ski area crowds, this private ski slope is the one for you, a real Pacific Northwest treasure. Open only on weekends. *mountaineers.org*

Stevens Pass

Stevens was proudly scruffy and local with a robust RV parking lot culture until 2018, when Vail Resorts bought it. But with the buyout came upgrades and tentative plans for expansion. Stevens has a lot to love, like the exceptional fall-line runs on the back side and plenty of advanced slopes. There's still a parking area for RVs, but it's cleaned up now and available by reservation only, with no overflow parking allowed.

Leavenworth Ski Hill

Downhill ski a few miles from downtown Leavenworth at this small but pleasant ski hill. With two rope tows, a Nordic jumping hill with ski jumping tournaments, and night skiing, it's good fun for the whole family. The historic 1936 lodge is available to rent for private gatherings.

SLEDDING AND TUBING

Hyak Sno-Park (Snoqualmie)

The groomed hills and heated restrooms make this a popular winter place to sled and tube. You'll need a Sno-Park pass to park here and a special groomed trails permit. Dogs are not allowed. No amenities, so bring everything you'll need: sled, picnic, and water.

Summit Tubing Center (Snoqualmie)

At the peak of the season, the tubing center has over 20 lanes of groomed snow to slide down for 2-hour slots; a conveyor belt tows you back to the top. All this and a tube for the price of a ticket. Open Friday through Sunday during the season. Make reservations online. *summitatsnoqualmie.com*

Lt. Michael Adams Tubing Park (Leavenworth)

This tubing hill is named for a local young man who graduated from West Point and was killed in 2004 while serving in Iraq. Friends and family donated the funds as a way to honor him, a unique and poignant tribute. A rope tow pulls tubers up the 100-foot hill. A tube is provided with the price of a ticket. Birthday alert: the tubing hill is available for private parties.

ICE-SKATING RINKS

Kahler Glen Ice Rink (Leavenworth)

It's big. It's uncrowded. It's free. This dreamy ice rink is the real deal: a 14,000-square-foot flooded driving range pond that has a variety of hockey and figure skates available on-site for people to use for free. Off of Highway 2, it's 20 miles north of Leavenworth. *avada.lakewenatcheeinfo.com/kahler-glen-ice-rink-conditions*

Leavenworth Ice Rink

The rink is located in downtown Leavenworth and surrounded by Cascade peaks that make you feel you're on a movie set as you slide and twirl. Price of admission includes skates. *leavenworth.org/experience/ice-skating*

Suncadia Resort (Snoqualmie)

The outdoor rink is for guests only, so you'll have to make reservations to stay here if you want to skate. Ice skate at night and warm yourself up beside the fire pit afterward.

EXPLORE MORE ADVENTURES

Fat Bike This Trail at Night

A fat bike is basically a mountain bike with really fat tires and low air pressure for more tire coverage to grip snow (and sand), allowing you to conquer any terrain. It's a growing trend that will extend your cycling season. Rent one in Leavenworth at Arlberg Sports Haus. Try it up Icicle Creek Road during the day, but at night the Leavenworth Ski Hill allows them on the Nordic trails between 6:00 and 10:00 p.m.

Take an Avalanche Safety Course

If you want to expand your backcountry skills, or snowshoe off-piste, or just feel more comfortable in the snow, it's critical to have a good understanding of avalanches. Up your outdoor game with a Mountain Madness introductory class that includes 2 field days. *mountainmadness.com*

Go on a Dogsled Ride

Need an uplift of joy? Go on a dogsled ride. The dogs yip and wriggle and thrill with eagerness to begin the pull, and their energy and enthusiasm will fill you up to spilling over. There's only one company in the state of Washington that will take you, and that's Northwest Dogsled Adventures. Rides begin at the Fish Lake/Lake Wenatchee trailhead. They fill fast, so make your reservation early; you won't regret it. *northwestdogsledadventuresllc.com*

MOUNT RAINIER, WASHINGTON

Mount Rainier, Washington

Tahoma

Sixty miles south of Seattle, Mount Rainier (also known by its Native name, Tahoma) dominates the horizon with imposing majesty. On clear days it can be seen as far north as Victoria, Canada, and as far south as Corvallis, Oregon. On those fine days we point to the looming 14,411-foot stratovolcano as if seeing it for the first time. A Tahoma view day is a good day in the Pacific Northwest, but underneath the mountain's cool and elegant presence is a seething interior. There's a high probability of eruption in the near future, and it's been placed on the Decade Volcanoes list with 15 others across the world for having the greatest probability of causing significant loss of life and property damage if eruptive activity progresses. The danger lies in the fact that Tahoma is the most heavily glaciated peak in the continental United States, with 36 square miles of glaciers and permanent snowfields. When Mount St. Helens' lateral blast melted the ice fields in 1980, huge torrents of mud and water flowed within *seconds* down river valleys. With more ice to melt on Rainier, and its proximity to urban areas, an eruption would decimate the region.

But even with the mountain's past violent outbursts, humans have taken advantage of its abundant biodiversity and resources. Tahoma is a rich site for Indigenous people's culture, with archeological evidence going back at least 9,000 years. Named by Salishan speakers as Tahoma, or Tacoma, meaning "Mother of Waters," the mountain continues to be a spiritual place for Native Americans. For millennia the ancestors of today's tribes—the Nisqually, Squaxin Island, Muckleshoot, Yakama, Cowlitz, and Puyallup—came to hunt and gather resources on all sides of the mountain. The construction of Mount Rainier National Park excluded Indigenous peoples, but today a growing awareness of their deep roots at Tahoma is shifting public perspective, and with it an effort to restore equity.

Mount Rainier National Park is huge, at over 369 square miles, with 260 miles of maintained trails within its boundaries, including the epic and grueling 93-mile Wonderland Trail, which circles the flanks of the mountain. The magnificent Spray Park section of the trail is featured

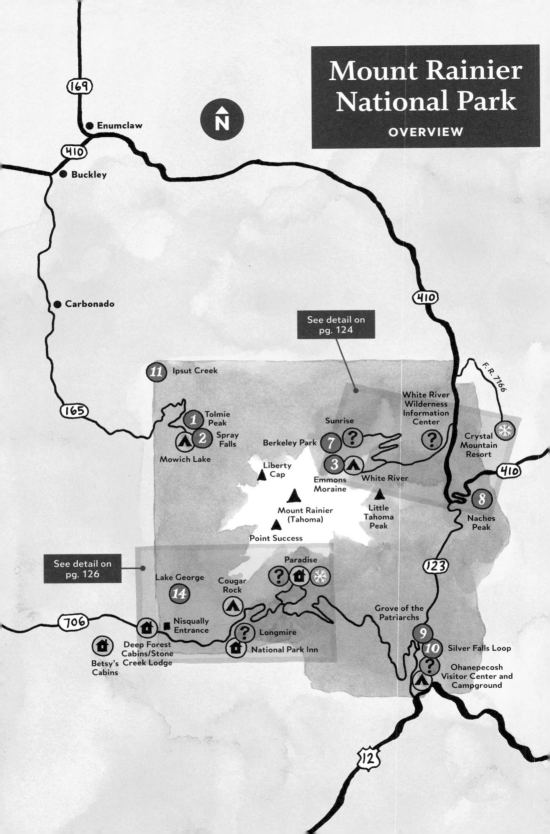

Mount Rainier
National Park
OVERVIEW

169

● Enumclaw

410

● Buckley

● Carbonado

410

F.R. 7166

See detail on
pg. 124

11 Ipsut Creek

165

1 Tolmie
Peak

2 Spray
Falls

Mowich Lake

Liberty
Cap

Berkeley Park

Sunrise

7 ?

3

Emmons
Moraine

White River
Wilderness
Information
Center

?

❄ Crystal
Mountain
Resort

410

White River

Little
Tahoma
Peak

8

Naches
Peak

Mount Rainier
(Tahoma)

Point Success

See detail on
pg. 126

Lake George

14

Nisqually
Entrance

Cougar
Rock

Paradise

? 🏠 ❄

123

Grove of the
Patriarchs

706

? Longmire

National Park Inn

Deep Forest
Cabins/Stone
Creek Lodge

Betsy's
Cabins

9

10 Silver Falls Loop

? Ohanepecosh
Visitor Center and
Campground

12

on page 125. As you will have paid your fee upon entrance or used your America the Beautiful Pass, there are no other passes needed for the hikes other than a wilderness permit if you overnight in the backcountry. Note that pets are not allowed on hikes, only on leashes in designated campgrounds.

There are four main entrances to the park: Carbon River in the northwest, White River/Sunrise in the northeast, Stevens Canyon in the southeast, and Nisqually in the southwest. Nisqually is the only entrance open year-round; the others are closed in winter. Keep in mind over 2.3 million people come to Mount Rainier National Park every year, making it one of the most visited national parks in the United States. Plan for big crowds in high summer and on weekends, and if possible, come in September, still a glorious time. No matter the season or the crowds, as you hike through meadow seas of wildflowers to glaciers and vibrant valleys, you'll find the mountain beckoning before you, a mountain like no other.

Get Away

CAMPGROUNDS ▲

Mowich Lake

This is the smallest and perhaps the most stunning of the park's campgrounds with 13 walk-in, first-come, first-served campsites alongside Mowich Lake. The sites are located a short walk from the parking lot at the end of a rough 3-mile road. It's a resupply camp for weary Wonderland Trail hikers and the campground is free, so scoring a campsite here during high summer can be difficult. No campfires; closed in winter; no pets allowed.

White River ♿

Located in the northeastern section of the park, White River is a first-come, first-served campground that offers a stellar gateway for your mountain adventures. You will encounter climbers attempting to summit Mount Rainier by the east route, Wonderland Trail hikers, and car-camping families at this 112-site campground. The high elevation (4,232 feet) and the snow accumulation here make this campground the last to open in summer and the first to close for the winter. Pets allowed on leashes.

Ohanapecosh ♿

Located beside the crystal-clear waters of the Ohanapecosh River, this campground is the park's largest. Named by the Upper Cowlitz tribe, Ohanapecosh is believed to mean "standing at the edge." There are 195 individual sites set among an old-growth forest with several family-friendly hiking trailheads within walking distance, including the Ohanapecosh Hot Springs Trail (the hot springs are shallow silty pools not fit for soaking) and the Silver Falls Loop (Hike #10). A visitor center on the grounds offers more information on the natural and cultural history of the area. Some sites are available first come, first served, but make reservations if possible. Pets allowed on leashes; closed in winter.

Cougar Rock ♿

This large campground in the southwest corner of the park near Longmire and Paradise has 173 well-spaced individual sites and 5 group sites. A small number of sites are first come, first served, but reservations are highly recommended at this popular campground. Pets allowed on leashes; closed in winter.

CABINS AND LODGES 🏠

Betsy's Cabins at Mount Rainier

Luxe cabins with hot tubs, fireplaces, and outdoor fire pits. The cabins can accommodate from 2 to 10 people. Close to Longmire; open year-round. Bring your snowshoes in winter. *cabinsatrainier.com*

Stone Creek Lodge

Reasonably priced cabins just 200 yards from the Nisqually entrance, which is the park's main entrance and the only one open year-round. The cabins have hot tubs, gas fireplaces, and kitchenettes. Open year-round. *stonecreeklodge.net*

Deep Forest Cabins

These are lovely cabins, most sited privately in a forest with full kitchens, gas fireplaces, and hot tubs to soak in after long hikes. It's a 12-mile drive to Longmire and the Mount Rainier playground. Open year-round. *deepforestcabins.com*

National Park Inn ♿

The inn is rustic, but it's located a short drive from the Paradise area, making it a good base for hikes. There is no Wi-Fi, cell service, or televisions, but there is a great fireplace in the guest library and magnificent views of Mount Rainier on the veranda. Closed in winter. *mtrainierguestservices.com*

Paradise Inn ♿

It's all about the mountain. You'll spend little time in your small but clean room, and there is no cell service or Wi-Fi. So go outside; this is one of the most beautiful settings you will ever stay in. Closed in winter. *mtrainierguestservices.com*

Season of Green

DAY HIKES

1. Tolmie Peak Lookout/Eunice Lake ♂ ⚙ 🐾 ✨

- Moderate
- 7.5 miles round trip out and back
- 1,100 feet elevation gain
- 4.5 hours

This gorgeous hike has a little bit of everything the park has to offer: an exquisite lake, a wildflower-filled meadow, a view of North Mowich Glacier, a relatively easy summit of a peak, and a 360-degree vista from the top, straight out of a movie set. The trailhead is on the west side of Mowich Lake. *wta.org*

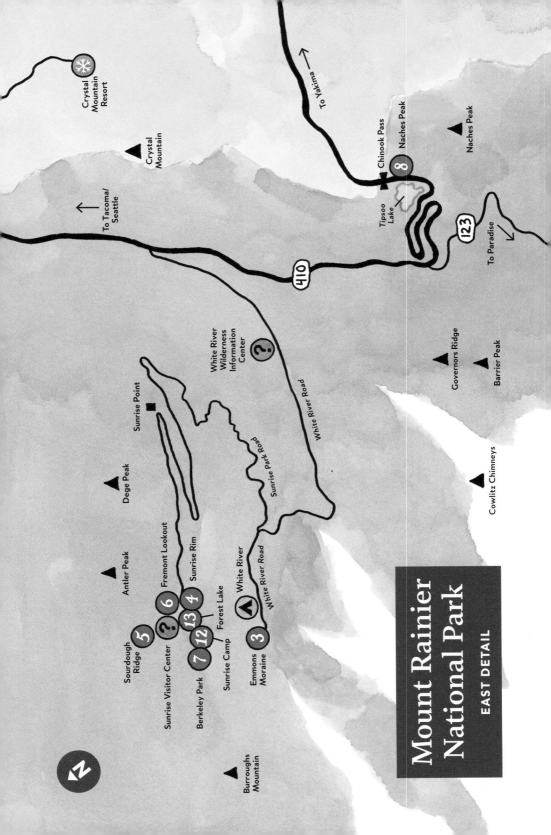

Crystal Mountain Resort

Crystal Mountain

To Tacoma/ Seattle

To Yakima

Chinook Pass

Naches Peak

8

Naches Peak

Tipsoo Lake

123

To Paradise

410

White River Wilderness Information Center

?

White River Road

Governors Ridge

Barrier Peak

Sunrise Point

Sunrise Park Road

Dege Peak

Cowlitz Chimneys

Antler Peak

Fremont Lookout

Sunrise Rim

White River Road

White River

3

Forest Lake

Sourdough Ridge

5

Sunrise Visitor Center

6

?

13

4

12

7

Berkeley Park

Sunrise Camp

Emmons Moraine

N

Burroughs Mountain

Mount Rainier National Park

EAST DETAIL

2. Spray Falls and Spray Park ☺ ⚲ ⚙ ✂ 🐾 ✨ ♨

- Easy to Spray Falls/Moderate to Spray Park
- 4 miles round trip out and back to Spray Falls/8 miles round trip out and back to Spray Park
- Negligible elevation gain to Spray Falls/1,700 feet to Spray Park
- 2 hours to Spray Falls/4–5 hours to Spray Park

Full of unfurling views, bedazzling, wildflower heavy—there is no way to fully describe this breathtaking hike. The first 2 miles to Spray Falls, a spectacular veiled horsetail that twists and drops a total of 354 feet, are easy with rolling hills and little to no elevation gain. From here the creaky-kneed and very young may want to turn back, while others can hike on for 2 miles and climb a series of grueling switchbacks that bring you panting and awestruck to the best views of the entire hike: one unfolding meadow after another with Echo and Observation Rocks, and of course the grande dame Mount Rainier, in the background. From here keep your eye out for a spur trail on the left that leads to Mist Park; drink in the view, then return to Mowich Lake. Be a pro hiker and stick to the trails: do *not* venture out into the meadows for a better view. It takes years for this fragile ecosystem to repair. *wta.org*

3. Emmons Moraine ⚲ ✨

- Easy to moderate
- 3 miles round trip out and back
- 900 feet elevation gain
- 1.5–2 hours

The Emmons Glacier is impressive, covering the largest area of any glacier in the Lower 48, stretching for over 4 miles from its start high on the peak of Mount Rainier down to the milky headwaters of the White River. You'll see the terminal snout of the glacier covered in rocks as the White River gushes from beneath it. Note that this would be a family-friendly hike except near the end, where there's a short and pitched ascent from the river crossing to the ridge that overlooks Emmons. The footing is loose, and the path changes every year. Use good judgment. *wta.org*

4. Sunrise Rim ☺ ⚙ ✨

- Easy
- 5-mile loop
- 840 feet elevation gain
- 3 hours

If you can't get enough glacier gazing, this is your hike! The easy hike leads up to the first bump of Burroughs Mountain for a spectacular view of

Mount Rainier National Park

SOUTH DETAIL

N

Mazama Ridge

Panorama Point

Paradise Inn

Henry M. Jackson Visitor Center

Nisqually Vista

Alta Vista

Stevens Canyon Road

Pinnacle Peak

Wahpenayo Peak

Rixksecker Point

Cougar Rock

Longmire Wilderness Information Center

National Park Inn

Glacier Island

Pyramid Peak

Copper Mountain

Lake George

14

Westside Road

Mount Wow

Paradise Road

706

Nisqually Entrance

Deep Forest Cabins

Stone Creek Lodge

Mount Rainier and her necklace of glaciers. Along the way you'll also pass Sunrise Camp, a small backcountry camp that makes an excellent base for further hikes, and Shadow Lake. Because the hike is at a high elevation, snow may cover the trail well into July. Always check road and trail conditions before leaving. *alltrails.com*

5. Sourdough Ridge Trail ☺ ✿ ☀

- Easy
- 2.5 miles round trip out and back
- 400 feet elevation gain
- 1 hour

This undemanding trail is short and satisfying. The start is a bit north from the Sunrise Visitor Center up a wide set of stairs and heads into the green valley of Yakima Park. The trail offers striking views as you make your way across the ridge to a five-way intersection. Here, you can turn around and return to the parking lot, or there are multiple options for continued hiking: to Dege (pronounced "Deh-gay") Peak, Forest Lake, Berkeley Park, or Burroughs Mountain. *wta.org*

6. Fremont Lookout ✿ ☀

- Moderate
- 5.6 miles round trip out and back
- 1,200 feet elevation gain
- 3.5–4 hours

There's very little shade and no water on this hike, but plenty of jaw-dropping views. When you arrive at the beautifully restored lookout tower, gaze out at a visual overload of mountains and valleys. A sunrise hike here is memorable. *wta.org*

7. Berkeley Park ✿ 🌿 ☀ ♨

- Moderate
- 7.7 miles round trip out and back
- 1,700 feet elevation gain
- 4–5 hours

No wildflower hikes can compare to the vast explosions of form, color, and variety of flowers in Berkeley Park. During the wildflower season, virtually every square inch of the huge meadows are covered in blossoms. Lodi Creek runs beside the trail and plays a musical score for the scene. Stop to picnic or soak your feet in the cold current. Keep your eyes out for American water dippers. *wta.org*

front and center as you hike. Wait until late July or early August (early autumn is even better!)—the eastern slopes of the peak can hold snow late into the summer season and you'll need snow and ice footwear traction and trekking poles before it melts. Because of the crowds, plan to come midweek or in the early autumn. *wta.org*

9. Grove of the Patriarchs ☺ ♀ ★

- Easy
- 1.5 miles round trip out and back
- 50 feet elevation gain
- 1 hour

This is an unforgettable hike for tree aficionados—some trees here are over a thousand years old. The gentle trail follows the Ohanapecosh River, then crosses on a cool suspension bridge to an island where the trees tower above you. Informative interpretive signs along the boardwalk explain the rich complexity of an old-growth forest. Don't miss this one! *wta.org*

10. Silver Falls Loop ☺ ♀ 🐾 ♨

- Easy
- 3-mile loop
- 600 feet elevation gain
- 1.5 hours

The Ohanapecosh River has some of the clearest water of any river in the park because its source is snowmelt, not a glacier with its accompanying silt. The current runs down in a series of progressively larger cascades and ends in a powerful 40-foot plunge into a jade-green pool. This easy loop begins and ends in the Ohanapecosh campground, and you can hike further on the moderate Eastside Trail if desired. *wta.org*

MULTIDAY BACKPACKING

All wilderness permits required for the following hikes are available in person at the park's visitor center or in advance from *recreation.gov /permits/4675317.*

11. Ipsut Creek Backcountry Campground ☺ ✿ ⚯ ❦ ♨

- Wilderness permit
- Easy
- 10 miles round trip out and back
- 700 feet elevation gain
- 5.5 hours

After a flood in 2006, sections of the Carbon River Road were washed out, so the park converted it to a foot and bicycle trail, with no vehicle access past the park entrance boundary. What was once a car campground is now a backcountry destination and a perfect place for a base. You can get the backcountry permit from the Carbon River Ranger Station, then hike 5 miles on the road to make camp. You have a choice of several hikes in the following day(s): Ipsut Falls, the Wonderland Trail to Mowich Lake, and the Carbon River trail. If possible, hike to Carbon Glacier. *alltrails.com*

12. Sunrise Camp ☺ ✿ ✸

- Wilderness permit
- Easy
- 2.6 miles round trip out and back
- 275 feet elevation gain
- 1.5 hours

It can be difficult to reserve a permit at this small campground (7 walk-in sites), but it's a perfect first-time backpacker's trip and popular with families. Trails from here include Berkeley Park (Hike #7), Burroughs Mountain, Frozen Lake, Sourdough Ridge (Hike #5), and Fremont Lookout (Hike #6). Bring a water filtration or purification system; your water source is nearby Shadow Lake. *alltrails.com*

13. Forest Lake ☺ ✿ ⚯ ❦

- Wilderness permit
- Easy to moderate
- 5 miles round trip out and back
- 1,300 feet elevation gain
- 4 hours

The pros: the trail is uncrowded, passes through lush meadows of wildflowers, has 1 private campsite on the lake, and offers plentiful wildlife viewing, including pikas, mountain goats, and elk. The cons: the trail is rocky in sections; after a brief initial ascent it's all downhill to the lake, but you'll have an unrelenting climb out. Be prepared for some whining from little ones on the return, and like on all mountain lake hikes in summer, there will be mosquitoes. Bring bug spray. *wta.org*

14. Lake George ☺ ⚘ ♨

- Wilderness permit
- Easy to moderate
- 9.2 miles round trip out and back
- 930 feet elevation gain
- 5 hours

This used to be one of the most popular and crowded hikes in the park until the Westside Road was decommissioned; now it's yours with far fewer people. The slowly ascending 3.8-mile hike up the Westside Road allows side-by-side walking and good conversation with your hiking buddy, nothing special but it will get you to the Lake George trailhead. Take the short but steep-ish hike to beautiful Lake George and your camp. The next morning, hike Gobblers Knob to the fire lookout perched upon fists of stone. *wta.org*

EXPLORE MORE ADVENTURES

Forage for Mushrooms

The forests around Mount Rainier hold troves of edible mushrooms, from chanterelles to matsutake (pine mushrooms) and more for those who can positively identify them. Always go with an experienced guide if you are new to harvesting, or join a mycological club, such as Puget Sound Mycological Society, to familiarize yourself with identifying and finding the edible mushrooms of the Pacific Northwest. Most fall species emerge after the first seasonal rain. Watch the weather, then head to the hiking trails off of State Route 410 for abundant chanterelle picking. Use proper harvest practices and cut the stem at ground level or slightly above with a knife. Special permits to harvest mushrooms are required from the US Forest Service (USFS). *apps.fs.usda.gov/gp*

WILD BERRIES

BLACKBERRY

SALAL BERRY

THIMBLEBERRY

SALMONBERRY

BLUEBERRY

HUCKLEBERRY

OREGON GRAPE

Horseback Ride the Back Trails

Guided trail rides are a different way to experience the mountains. Echo River Ranch near Enumclaw offers guided rides that are always done at a walk, perfect for beginner riders. EZ Times Horse Rides, located farther south near Elbe, has sunset trail rides and can match the rider's experience to the horse. *echoriverranch.com; eztimeshorserides.com*

All Together Now: Take a Family Mountain Bike Ride

Mountain biking to delightful Packwood Lake is an easy ride for the whole family. Pack a picnic and enjoy it by the shore before returning. From the gated area at FSR 066, go 3.2 miles to a four-way intersection; continue straight, then it's 4.3 miles to Packwood Lake. *visitrainier.com*

Hike from the Crystal Mountain Gondola

For a fun alternative to the usual hike, drive to Crystal Mountain and take the gondola up to the summit for a wide variety of trails to choose from. The view of Mount Rainier from the top is postcard perfect. Have lunch and a brew at the Summit House after hiking, then save your knees and take the gondola back down. Pets allowed on leashes.

Mountain Bike Carbon River Road

Mount Rainier National Park has given up trying to repair Carbon River Road: the Carbon River won after repeated washouts and floods. The good news is cycling the carved-up road—with its gentle elevation gain, passable creeks, and random rocky terrain—makes an interesting and very doable mountain-bike trip. The first half along the river is peaceful; the rest will keep you alert. The 5 miles to Ipsut Creek Backcountry Campground for lunch makes a great day. *visitrainier.com*

Season of Snow

The southwest entrance to the park, Nisqually, is the only entrance open in winter, but even it closes in extreme weather. Always check road conditions before leaving. The road between Longmire and the Paradise area—your center for snow adventures—closes nightly for snow removal and reopens in the morning, barring extreme weather. All cars, including 4WD and AWD, are required to bring chains into the park. Avalanche danger is always an issue in regions like Mount Rainier that receive high snowfall, especially on the steeper trails. Stop at the Nisqually entrance for a paper guide to the areas of avalanche concern for the safest approaches on the trails.

SNOWSHOE AND CROSS-COUNTRY SKI TRAILS

Guided Snowshoe Trip

Guided walks in the Paradise area are offered at the Henry M. Jackson Visitor Center on a first-come, first-served basis, usually on Saturdays, Sundays, and holidays. Sign-ups are available 1 hour before the trip. Check ahead; there are no guided trips when the visitor center is closed. Snowshoes are included but are to be used only for the guided trip. If you need snowshoes for the day, rent them at the Longmire General Store (cross-country skis are also available). The following easy trails leave from Paradise and work for both snowshoeing and cross-country skiing. For more, check out the map of winter trails at *npmaps.com/wp-content /uploads/mount-rainier-paradise-winter-trails-map.gif.*

Alta Vista

This 1.5-mile round-trip snowshoe is a good beginner's route with only 560 feet of elevation gain. The trail is usually packed down from skis and snowshoe tracks and easy to follow. The views are dreamy from here, and on clear days you'll see Mount Rainier's volcano cousins Mount Adams and Mount St. Helens. *wta.org/go-hiking/hikes/alta-vista-loop*

Panorama Point

You'll sweat on this trail even in winter, but not too much: it's only 5 miles round trip, and the panoramic vista from the top is exquisite. Take your time, take photos, and watch the skiers and snowboarders whoosh down from the point after hiking up. *wta.org*

Mazama Ridge

This easy 6-mile round-trip trail does not disappoint! Mazama Ridge trail is a winter wonderland of snowy alpine meadows, with wide views from the ridge, but it can be prone to avalanches. Be sure to check with the rangers about the danger level before leaving. *wta.org*

Nisqually Vista Trail

This straightforward 1-mile loop trail is the biggest bang for your buck from Paradise. It brings you to a magnificent vista from the Nisqually Glacier overlook above the Nisqually River. *wta.org*

DOWNHILL SKI AND SNOWBOARD TRIPS

Crystal Mountain

Crystal Mountain is the largest ski resort in Washington, with 2,600 acres, over 50 runs, and 11 lifts. It caters to the intermediate to advanced skier and snowboarder, but snow bunnies will find slopes to plow too. There are three slope-side accommodations—the Alpine Inn, the Village Inn, and Quicksilver Lodge—and an RV parking lot with hookups.

SLEDDING AND TUBING

Snowplay Area at Paradise

This is the only place in the national park where sledding is allowed, but with several chutes built and maintained by USFS, there is plenty of room to play. It opens when 5 feet of snow covers the fragile ecosystem below, typically late December to mid-March. Bring your own tube or saucer; no rigid sleds or toboggans allowed. *nps.gov*

EXPLORE MORE ADVENTURES

Ski or Snowshoe Hut to Hut

Volunteers with the Mount Tahoma Trails Association operate and manage 50 miles of trails just southwest of Mount Rainier National Park that include three ski huts and a yurt. The huts are available for overnights by permit only, but the common kitchen and dining areas are available for day skiers and snowshoers. A volunteer will haul your gear up by pulk (a sled without runners) for a donation. *skimtta.org*

SLED TYPES

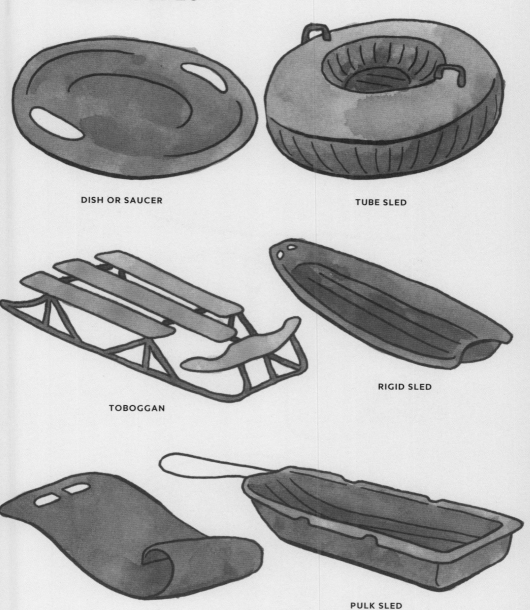

DISH OR SAUCER

TUBE SLED

TOBOGGAN

RIGID SLED

ROLL-UP OR CARPET

PULK SLED

BUILD A QUINZEE

Snow Camp: Build a Quinzee

Mount Rainier National Park is mantled with deep snow in winter, and camping is a unique adventure if you're prepared. It's allowed almost everywhere once the snowpack reaches 2 feet (5 feet at Paradise to protect vegetation). You need to be 300 feet from plowed roads and 100 feet from water sources, and you'll need a backcountry permit from the Longmire Wilderness Information Center or the Henry M. Jackson Visitor Center. Ready? Build a quinzee for a cozy camp shelter. The quinzee originated with the Athabascans, an Alaska Interior tribe, and is essentially a giant pile of snow that you hollow out to create a shelter. Quinzees are not difficult to build; you just need the right snow conditions, teamwork, and patience. Here's the test: Can you make a snowball? If it doesn't stick together, wait for another day, but if it does, you're in luck. Grab your fellow adventurers and start shoveling!

1. Make a pile of snow at least 5 feet high (even better, 6 or 7 feet high) and big enough around to hold two prone people. This will take a long time. Allow the snow to set for an hour or two to sinter (or compact)—the longer the better. This is key to the integrity of the quinzee. Snowflakes have thin points radiating from a central node, and when you shovel and mix them, the points break off and the snowflakes bond. You can push the process along by flipping the snow while shoveling it onto the pile. After an hour or two, it's time. Shape an entrance from the pile, then poke foot-long sticks or skewers all over the big mound as a guide for wall depth as you dig.
2. Using a large trowel or a dustpan, hollow out the entrance. Crawl in, then slowly work inward and upward, throwing the snow out behind you to let others clear it away. Take care not to dig too deep and puncture the snow walls; the sticks will be your guide when you've reached the proper thickness.
3. Keep a small shovel inside at night in case you need to dig out from a snowstorm in the morning. It took a lot of work to make, so you'd better spend several nights here.

MOUNT ST. HELENS, WASHINGTON

Mount St. Helens, Washington

Loowit

Before it erupted in May of 1980, the youngest of the major Cascade volcanoes, Mount St. Helens, had the silhouette of an iconic cone. It was even referred to as the Mount Fuji of America, but all that changed on May 18, 1980. After several months of intense activity earlier in the spring—including more than 10,000 earthquakes and a significant expansion of the entire north flank—an earthquake beneath the volcano triggered the northern bulge into a violent slide, creating the largest terrestrial landslide in recorded history. Almost immediately after the landslide began, a gigantic lateral blast of hot gas, steam, ash, and molten rock—some the size of cars—followed, sweeping across the region at up to 680 miles per hour. Forests were scorched and snowfields and glaciers melted, creating massive floods that raced down river valleys. The lateral blast destroyed an area the size of Chicago in 180 *seconds* and reduced the summit height by 1,300 feet. Stratovolcanoes like Mount St. Helens are prone to erupt explosively and cause considerable risk to life and infrastructure, whereas the flatter, broader shield volcanoes, like those in Hawaii, ooze lava from their vents, causing damage but little loss of life.

In 1982, Congress designated the immediate area around Mount St. Helens as a national volcanic monument, protecting it for scientific research, education, and public recreation. Today volcanic activity is not imminent, but the mountain is young, volatile, and still active. Mount St. Helen's Native name, Loowit, or "Lady of Fire," is shortened from longer names given to the mountain by various local tribes, and reflects the mountain's eruptive nature throughout human history. Through centuries of oral history the tribes passed on knowledge of the periodic fiery explosions, and this knowledge has contributed to the geological record of the region.

The Loowit region can be less crowded than other mountain areas, in part because of the lack of campgrounds, services, and accommodations within the monument itself. But there are campgrounds within an hour's drive, and it's a fascinating, stunningly beautiful place to explore. Visit one of the visitor and interpretive centers to enhance your exploration:

- Mount St. Helens Visitor Center (at Seaquest/Silver Lake)
- Johnston Ridge Observatory (at the end of State Highway 504)

Mount St. Helens

OVERVIEW

To Randle

Iron Creek

F. R. 25

Lower Falls

Meta Lake

5

Spirit Lake

Goat Creek/ Cathedral Falls

4

Coldwater Lake

Harry's Ridge

3

2

?

Johnston Ridge Eruption Trail

Johnston Ridge Observatory

Riffe Lake

1

Hummocks Trail #229

Mount St. Helens

June Lake/ Pine Marten

6

Sasquatch Loop/ June Lake/Pine Marten/ Marble Mountain Sno-Park

❄

F. R. 90

Swift Reservoir

Butte Camp

9

Ape Cave

8

7

Trail of Two Forests Interpretive Site

Cougar

Yale Lake

503

Lake Merwin

Spirit Lake Highway

Silver Lake

504

Mount St. Helens Visitor Center

Seaquest State Park

?

Castle Rock

N

Longview

Kalama

5

Columbia River

Get Away

CAMPGROUNDS ▲

Seaquest State Park ♿

The park has 55 tent spaces, 33 hookup sites, and 5 yurts available to rent that sleep up to 5. Silver Lake is a short stroll away, and the Silver Lake Mount St. Helens Visitor Center, which offers naturalist-led hikes and interpretive exhibits, is within walking distance via a pedestrian tunnel. A great base for exploring and hiking. Open year-round; reservations required for sites and yurts; pets allowed on leashes.

Iron Creek ♿

It's a 90-minute drive to Mount St. Helens from this 99-site campground located near the confluence of Iron Creek and the Cispus River in an old-growth forest. It's volcano nation here with Mount Rainier to the north, Mount Adams (Klickitat) to the east, and Mount St. Helens to the west. The Woods Creek Watchable Wildlife Area is a 5-minute drive and has a wonderful interpretive trail. Closed in winter, but primitive camping at a few sites is available. Pets allowed on leashes.

Lower Falls ♿

There are 43 reservable, spacious sites for both tents and RVs up to 60 feet, with trails from the campground leading to the Lewis River and several impressive waterfalls worth hiking to. Pets allowed on leashes; closed in winter.

Season of Green

For all hikes in this section, check *wta.org* for directions and the latest beta information.

DAY HIKES

1. Hummocks ☺ ✿ 🐾

- Monument Pass
- Easy
- 2.7-mile loop
- 250 feet elevation gain
- 2.5 hours

This is a fascinating hike past hummocks formed by the 1980 eruption when avalanche debris surged down the north side of Mount St. Helens. The once-desolate landscape is now crowded with life—wildflowers, frogs, elk, beaver, and birds all signaling renewal.

2. Johnston Ridge Eruption Trail ☺ ✿ ☀ ♿

- Monument Pass
- Easy
- 0.6 mile round trip out and back
- 25 feet elevation gain
- 30–45 minutes

This short paved hike is accessible to all and offers spectacular views and interpretive kiosks to explain and give context to what you're looking at. Panoramic views across the pumice plains to the crater will make you shiver.

3. Harry's Ridge ✿ 🐾 ☀

- Monument Pass
- Easy to moderate
- 8.2 miles round trip out and back
- 970 feet elevation gain
- 5 hours

Plan on spending extra time on this classic, terrific ridge hike; you need a leisurely pace to appreciate it. The views are breathtaking, the wildflowers sublime, and you'll end up on a high, windy ridge with panoramic views of Mount Adams and Mount St. Helens in all their glory.

4. Goat Creek/Cathedral Falls ☺ ⚙ 🦆 ♨ 🐾

- Northwest Forest Pass
- Easy to moderate
- 11 miles round trip out and back
- 400 feet elevation gain
- 6 hours

Prepare for the 4-mile potholed road that takes you to this trail, where caves, creek crossings, and magnificent Cathedral Falls await. The alcove behind the falls gives the waterfall its name.

5. Meta Lake ☺ ⚙ 🦆 ♿

- Northwest Forest Pass
- Easy
- 0.4-mile loop
- 10 feet elevation gain
- 30 minutes

The timing was right for this small valley. When the 1980 eruption occurred, this area was under 8 feet of snow, sparing small plants and animals from the searing lateral blast. The basin was scorched, but the recovery was swifter here than in more exposed areas. It's a landscape in robust transition. The trail circles the lake and brings you to a viewing platform, often underwater in the spring and early summer from snowmelt. Just east of the trailhead a path leads to Miner's Car, a car destroyed in the lateral blast, a visual reminder of nature's power.

6. June Lake ☺ ⚙ 🏊 🦆 ♨

- Northwest Forest Pass
- Easy
- 2.8 miles round trip out and back
- 445 feet elevation gain
- 1.5 hours

This small picturesque lake is nestled against a looming andesite cliff with a plunging 74-foot waterfall at one end. With cool clear water, the lake is a fine place to swim on hot sunny days. There are also many picnic sites around the shore that make good rest stops.

MOUNT ST. HELENS, WASHINGTON

7. Trail of Two Forests ☺ ♿

- Northwest Forest Pass
- Easy
- 0.5-mile loop
- 50 feet elevation gain
- 30–45 minutes

On this interpretive stroll you'll learn the geological history of the region through two distinct forests, one of which was consumed by lava 2,000 years ago, leaving remarkable tree lava casts behind. You can even climb down into one of them and explore it from the inside out.

8. Ape Caves ☺ (lower only) 🌟

- Northwest Forest Pass
- Easy to Lower Ape Cave Trail/ Moderate to difficult to Upper Ape Cave Trail
- 1.5 miles round trip to lower cave/2.6 miles round trip to upper cave
- 360 feet elevation gain to upper cave
- 1 hour to lower cave/2.5 hours to upper cave

Make it a 10-point wow—this is a most unusual hike. The Ape Caves—named after a group of exploring foresters in the 1950s who called themselves the St. Helens Apes—are divided into two caves. The Lower Ape Cave is an easy and family-friendly exploration that will thrill kids as they imagine entering the belly of a beast. The more difficult Upper Ape Cave requires physical agility and involves more climbing and scrambling than hiking, but you'll return by trail aboveground. It's the longest lava tube in the continental US, measuring at over 2 miles, and it's dark. Each person needs a headlamp and/or flashlight (and extra batteries); the lava tube is drippy, so bring rain gear. The tube is a constant 42 degrees year-round, so also bring an extra layer to wear.

MULTIDAY BACKPACKING

9. Butte Camp ✿ 🌿 🦋 ✨

- Northwest Forest Pass, wilderness permit self-issued at trailhead
- Easy to moderate
- 5 miles round trip out and back
- 957 feet elevation gain
- 3.5 hours

You'll start out crossing an old lava flow and then meander through a forested trail and pumiced meadows with great sweeps of wildflowers. The creek at Lower Butte Camp at 2.5 miles is your overnight destination and provides a fine base camp for day hikes. Try the short uphill hike to the Loowit Trail junction; Loowit Trail circumnavigates the base of the mountain.

EXPLORE MORE ADVENTURES

Visit the Mount St. Helens Institute

Forage for edible mushrooms and then prepare delectable dishes from them. Take a guided hike with a geologist into the crater. Bring the family to a multiday volcano adventure camp—all this and more from the Mount St. Helens Institute, which has wide-ranging offerings of educational programs and adventures. Through science camps, expert-led field seminars, and guided hiking explorations, the institute is dedicated to connecting people of all ages to the Pacific Northwest's youngest and most active volcano and the surrounding Gifford Pinchot National Forest. *mshinstitute.org*

Season of Snow

You're largely on your own at Mount St. Helens in winter; there are fewer services, less cell coverage, and less support than at other mountain areas and parks. Be a smart recreationist. Check the avalanche and weather forecast before heading out, and carry the 10 Essentials. *nwac.us*

SNOWSHOE AND CROSS-COUNTRY SKI TRAILS

Guided Snowshoe Trips

The Mount St. Helens Institute offers a variety of snowshoe trips across the mountain, guided by naturalists with extensive knowledge of the region. Most outings feature a natural wonder: an ice waterfall, frozen lakes, and gigantic volcanic rock bombs that flew on the blast and dropped from the sky.

Backcountry Trails from Marble Mountain Sno-Park

Marble Mountain Sno-Park, in the shadow of Mount St. Helens, has nearly 50 miles of multiuse trails shared by snowmobilers, snowshoers, and cross-country skiers. Note they're not groomed. The following trails are at the park. Visit the US Forest Service website to find a map. *fs.usda.gov/Internet /FSE_DOCUMENTS/stelprdb5288545.pdf*

June Lake

This is a gentle 5-mile snowshoe with several well-marked trail options. Pack a thermos of cocoa—at the lake you'll find a 74-foot plunge waterfall laced with icicles, and a bench to sit on while contemplating and sipping. It's a winter wonderland bliss moment. *wta.org*

Sasquatch Loop

The Sasquatch Trails are a series of winter trails near the south-facing flanks of the mountain. They're wide and well situated, away from avalanche zones, but you'll be sharing with snowmobiles on the Forest Service road sections of the trails. One of the interesting features of this snowshoe is the June Lake SNOTEL (elevation 3,440 feet)—not a place to spend the night, but an acronym for a remote backcountry weather station (see page 149). *hikeoftheweek.com/new/sasquatch-loop*

Pine Marten

This trail (labeled 245D on the map) runs parallel to Forest Road 83 and keeps you off the snowmobile highway as you make your way to June Lake. The trail ends 2 miles from the Sno-Park, but there you'll find a kiosk with a map and several other snowshoe trail options. *fs.usda.gov/Internet /FSE_DOCUMENTS/stelprdb5288545.pdf*

WHAT'S A SNOTEL?

SNOTEL is shorthand for Snowpack Telemetry, a backcountry weather station with automated sensors that measure data on precipitation, air temperature, the amount of water in the snow, and even more detailed information used in forecasting future water supplies. Most important to winter recreationists, it measures the depth of the snowpack and how much new snow has fallen. While most weather stations are located at airports far from mountain slopes, SNOTELS are on-site and more accurate. The real-time data is transferred via meteor burst communication. The sites transmit a radio signal 50 to 75 miles into the sky, where it bounces off a band of ionized meteorites. The ground station then catches the bounced signal and updates the information. The app Backcountry Beta gives you access to current snow conditions and the weather forecast from 730 SNOTEL sites in western Canada and the western United States. It's an excellent resource for winter sport enthusiasts.

CRATER LAKE, OREGON

PART 4
THE OREGON CASCADES

MOUNT HOOD REGION, OREGON

Mount Hood, Oregon

Wy'east

Another classically shaped stratovolcano in the Cascade Range, Mount Hood (called Wy'east by Native peoples) rises 11,244 feet, the highest point in Oregon. Native people have resided here for thousands of years and regard Wy'east, a mythical son of the Creator, as a sacred place. The many bands within the Chinook people developed a north-south trail system over the millennium that approximates the Pacific Crest Trail. You'll follow ancient Native routes when you hike the Wy'east area of the PCT in Oregon. The mountain was also a major landmark for the weary settlers who arrived on the Oregon Trail and skirted her southern flanks along the Barlow Trail, a difficult but much safer alternative to rafting down the treacherous Columbia River.

Sadly, the wildfires in the summer of 2020 significantly decimated much of Oregon's forestland. The hikes and outdoor adventures featured here are in areas that escaped most of the devastation and do not reflect the wide and varied outdoor opportunities that were available before the wildfire. The land will regenerate, but it will take time. Rain will promote new vegetation in the charred landscape: first wildflowers and grasses, then scrub trees. The regrowth will continue to progress through an ecological succession over the years to a final forest of climax trees—the woodlands we are familiar with. It's hard to imagine when we see vast acres of torched tree skeletons, but fire can be a force of renewal and a powerful metaphor of the continuation of life.

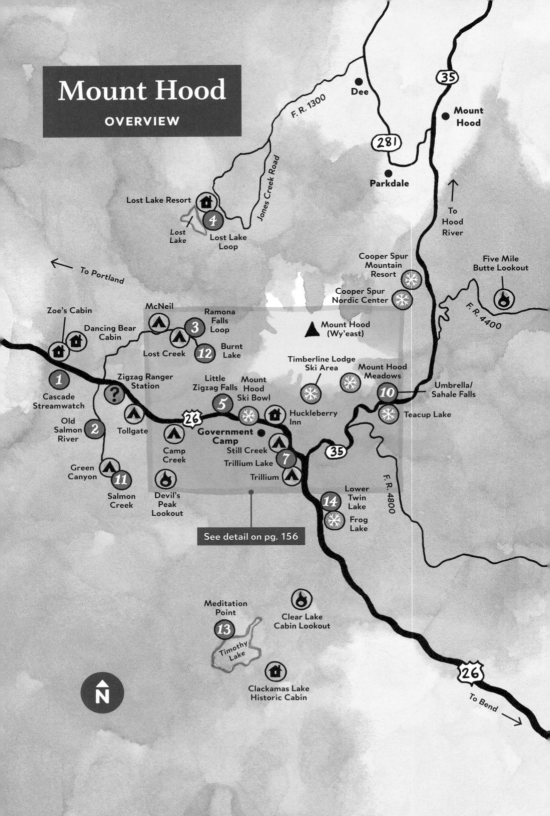

Mount Hood
OVERVIEW

Dee

Mount Hood

35

F.R. 1300

281

Parkdale

To Hood River

Lost Lake Resort

4

Lost Lake

Lost Lake Loop

Jones Creek Road

Cooper Spur Mountain Resort

Cooper Spur Nordic Center

Five Mile Butte Lookout

F.R. 4400

To Portland

Zoe's Cabin

Dancing Bear Cabin

McNeil

Ramona Falls Loop

3

Lost Creek

12

Burnt Lake

▲ Mount Hood (Wy'east)

Timberline Lodge Ski Area

Mount Hood Meadows

1

Cascade Streamwatch

Zigzag Ranger Station

?

Little Zigzag Falls

Mount Hood Ski Bowl

5

Umbrella/Sahale Falls

10

2

Old Salmon River

Tollgate

26

Camp Creek

Government Camp

Huckleberry Inn

Teacup Lake

Green Canyon

11

Salmon Creek

Devil's Peak Lookout

Still Creek

7

Trillium Lake

35

Trillium

See detail on pg. 156

14

Lower Twin Lake

F.R. 4800

Frog Lake

Meditation Point

13

Timothy Lake

Clear Lake Cabin Lookout

Clackamas Lake Historic Cabin

26

To Bend

N

Get Away

CAMPGROUNDS ▲

Green Canyon ♿

Green Canyon Campground is near many hiking trails in the Salmon-Huckleberry Wilderness area and the Wild and Scenic Salmon River. It's first come, first served with 15 campsites for RVs, trailers, and tents. Bring all the water you'll need; pets allowed on leashes; closed in winter.

Tollgate

This is one of the closest campgrounds to Portland and ideal headquarters for outdoor adventures in the Mount Hood region. Access hiking spots along the Oregon Trail and see a replica of the original Barlow Road tollgate east of the campground. The 10 reservable sites are closed in winter; pets allowed on leashes.

Camp Creek ♿

This CCC-built campground—old school, fabulous, and roomy—offers privacy other campgrounds don't have. It's a top camping spot with nearby hiking trails, berry picking, mushroom foraging, and bird-watching within reach of your campsite. There are 24 reservable sites; pets allowed on leashes; closed in winter.

Trillium Lake ♿

There are plenty of lakeside campsites at this family-friendly 62-site campground. The kids will enjoy fishing from a wheelchair-accessible pier, as well as swimming and hiking around the lake. Campfire programs are offered on weekends during the summer. Although there are a few first-come, first-served sites available, it's best to make reservations. Closed in winter, although the trail around the lake is popular with snowshoers during the snow season. Pets allowed on leashes.

Still Creek ♿

South of Mount Hood and near the charming town of Government Camp, Still Creek offers 27 reservable campsites in a meadow, with good fishing in the creek. Timberline Lodge ski area is nearby, and in the summer you can mountain bike, hike, or take a scenic chairlift ride there.

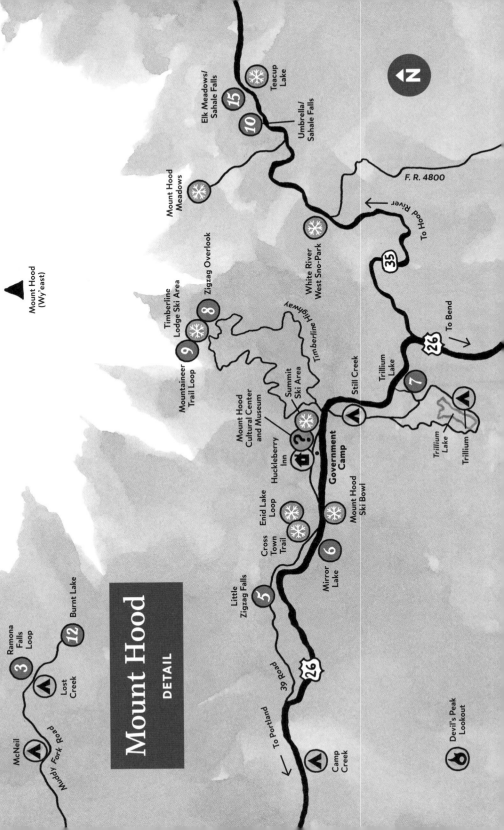

Mount Hood
DETAIL

N

Mount Hood (Wy'east)

To Portland

39 Road

US 26

Camp Creek

Devil's Peak Lookout

McNeil

Muddy Fork Road

Ramona Falls Loop

3

Lost Creek

12

Burnt Lake

Little Zigzag Falls

5

Cross Town Trail

Enid Lake Loop

6

Mirror Lake

Government Camp

Mount Hood Ski Bowl

Mount Hood Cultural Center and Museum

Huckleberry Inn

i ?

Summit Ski Area

Timberline Highway

Still Creek

Trillium Lake

7

Trillium Lake

Trillium

Mountaineer Trail Loop

9

Timberline Lodge Ski Area

8

Zigzag Overlook

White River West Sno-Park

To Bend

US 26

35

To Hood River

F. R. 4800

Mount Hood Meadows

Umbrella/ Sahale Falls

10

Elk Meadows/ Sahale Falls

15

Teacup Lake

McNeil

There are 35 open and sunny campsites along the Clear Fork of the Sandy River offered on a first-come, first-served basis. Although there is no potable water, there are other amenities, like fire rings and picnic tables, to make up for it. Check out the striking Ramona Falls while you're there, a moderate 7-mile round-trip hike (Hike #3). Pets allowed on leashes; closed in winter.

Lost Creek ♿

This is a fully accessible campground with a paved nature trail that wanders through the area. There are 14 reservable sites as well as 2 yurts accommodating up to 6 campers each. Pets allowed on leashes; closed in winter.

CABINS AND LODGES 🏠

Steiner Cabins: Zoe's and Dancing Bear

The cabins built by Henry Steiner and his family at the turn of the 20th century are architectural treasures straight out of a fairy tale, lovingly and carefully built by hand with local materials. The majority of the 100 they constructed are still standing nearly a hundred years later, and these are two you can rent.

Clackamas Lake Historic Cabin

Fair warning: Clackamas Lake Historic Cabin, operated by the US Forest Service (USFS), is notoriously difficult to reserve, but that doesn't mean it can't be yours! Clackamas is large enough to sleep eight people, but still cozy with a large stone fireplace and situated with outdoor opportunities steps away. The kitchen has a propane stove, a refrigerator, and cooking and eating utensils. There is hot and cold running water, but bring your own bedding. Open from Memorial Day through October.

Huckleberry Inn ♿

Smack in the middle of the fun town of Government Camp, the Huckleberry Inn is locally owned, family run, and offers 16 guest rooms as well as dorm-style accommodations for large groups. The attached Huckleberry Inn Restaurant serves classic burgers, soups, and (of course) huckleberry pie. Wi-Fi available for those who must connect technologically.

MOUNT HOOD REGION, OREGON

Timberline Lodge ♿

Now a national historic landmark, the lodge is an engineering feat built and funded by Franklin Roosevelt's Works Progress Administration program in 1936. It sits high on the base of Mount Hood, at 5,960 feet, and has a large accessible parking lot and ski-in, ski-out access for skiers and snowboarders. Even though the accommodations are resort-level expensive, and the rooms have thin walls and tiny bathrooms, staying here is worth it. The lodge is an icon on the skirt of a volcano.

Lost Lake Resort and Campground

Northwest of Mount Hood, the resort is a 2-hour drive from Portland with a plethora of water-based activities for young and old. Rent kayaks, canoes, paddleboards, or nonmotorized fishing boats at the general store, or trek around the numerous trails near the lake. There are many options for accommodations: yurts, cabins, rooms in the lodge, and a campground. It's popular! Make reservations early.

PACIFIC NORTHWEST LOOKOUTS

The fire lookouts of the Pacific Northwest were constructed in the early 20th century on high rugged peaks to discover and curb wildfires in vast tracts of wilderness. Before infrared devices, aerial technology, and livestreaming cameras, only the human eye could detect a fire, and those eyes proved very effective. Today there are hundreds of lookouts in Oregon and Washington, many of them decommissioned or in severe disrepair since technology has nudged them out of service. Many are still used for fire spotting, though, and 22 are available to the public for an exquisite overnight on top of the world. Think Jack Kerouac, Edward Abbey, and Gary Snyder, who romanced nature in solitude as they manned the fire towers for a summer. It's difficult to nail a reservation, though. Most lookouts are reservable 6 months in advance at *recreation.gov*, but the moment new dates open, they're often claimed by determined folks who push the button at the stroke of midnight. That person could be you.

LOOKOUTS

Fivemile Butte Lookout

It's a challenge to score a lookout reservation in Oregon, but try—Fivemile Butte is dreamy. In the summer you can drive up to the lookout, but in winter it's accessible only by skiing, snowshoeing, or snowmobiling 3 miles from the Billy Bob Sno-Park (permit required). There are 360-degree views from the four walls of windows, and on clear days you'll see Mounts Adams, Rainier, and St. Helens. Bring binoculars to scope out the abundant wildlife from the lookout and on the many trails available to hike from here, and bring all the water you'll need. *recreation.gov*

Clear Lake Cabin Lookout

Another popular winter lookout with stunning views, this lookout requires a pleasant 3.5-mile (one-way) snowshoe or ski trek. There's a woodstove for heat with firewood provided, which you'll need; this lookout is available only in winter. In the summer it's used by USFS. *recreation.gov*

Devil's Peak Lookout

You may have a chance to snag this one—Devil's Peak Lookout is first come, first served—but you'll pay for it with a 4-mile (one-way) grueling hike or snowshoe with 3,200 feet elevation gain from the Cool Creek trailhead. Because there are no reservations, you may make the trek and find the lookout occupied. Be prepared to hike on or back down. Bring plenty of water. *mountaineers.org*

Season of Green

For all of the following hikes, check out *oregonhikers.org* for directions and the latest beta information.

DAY HIKES

1. Cascade Streamwatch Loop ☺ ♀ 🦋 🐾 🌟 🏃

- America the Beautiful Pass or entrance fee
- Easy
- 5 miles or shorter, depending on the loop
- 40 feet elevation gain
- 3 hours

Located in the Wildwood Recreation Site, a public treasure run by the Bureau of Land Management, these loops and trails run through 580 acres of old-growth forest beside the pristine waters of the Wild and Scenic Salmon River. You'll find a wide variety of ecosystems with interpretive signs along boardwalks and wide paths, some paved and wheelchair accessible. The main not-to-miss attraction is the Cascade Streamwatch viewing pavilion, a fantastic underwater view of Sixes Creek, a salmon spawning creek where you can watch fingerling salmon hang out and feed. Don't miss this place! Open spring to early fall; pets allowed on leashes.

2. Old Salmon River ☺ ♀ ⚙ 🦋 🐾

- Northwest Forest Pass
- Easy
- 5 miles round trip out and back
- 200 feet elevation gain
- 2.5 hours

The Salmon River is pure and primal and designated Wild and Scenic for its entire 33-mile length. In some sections it pools lazily and in others it slams violently against canyon walls and smashes down steep waterfalls, making it famous among professional kayakers as the Mount Everest of Oregon kayaking. This hike offers the sweeter side of the Salmon River and is a lovely ramble filled with the sound of water moving over rocks. Near the turnaround after 2.5 miles, there is a great beach in the shade of cedars, perfect for a picnic before returning.

3. Ramona Falls Loop 🧍 ⚙ 🐦 🌟 〰

- Northwest Forest Pass
- Moderate
- 7.1 miles round trip out and back
- 1,100 feet elevation gain
- 4 hours

This moderate hike to the gorgeous Ramona Falls has a few tricky spots, including navigating a crossing of the Sandy River by either balancing on logs or fording in low-water months. A loop section of the trail follows the Pacific Crest Trail on the return, but before that your destination—Ramona Falls—awaits, like 100 feet of white lace draped across honeycomb-shaped columnar basalt.

4. Lost Lake Loop ☺ 🧍 ⚙ ✂ 🐦 🐾

- Day-use fee (pay at the kiosk in the north day-use parking lot)
- Easy
- 3.2-mile loop
- 60 feet elevation gain
- 1.5–2 hours

A fabulous hike for kids, this is a level trail with little elevation gain, a number of fishing piers, and a lake to play in. You can rent canoes, kayaks, fishing boats, and paddleboards at Lost Lake Campground. Lost Lake is said to be one of the most photographed lakes in Oregon—at the north end Mount Hood is reflected, shimmering and formidable, in the still water, especially beautiful at dawn and dusk. There are a few primitive campsites a short distance up the Huckleberry Mountain Trail turnoff, making an easy backpacking opportunity.

5. Little Zigzag Falls ☺ 🧍 ⚙ 🐾 〰

- Northwest Forest Pass
- Easy
- 1 mile round trip out and back
- 180 feet elevation gain

Take a pleasant stroll along Little Zigzag Creek, past a bog that in the spring holds a stretch of skunk cabbages, also known as swamp lanterns for their luminescent yellow bloom. The 41-foot steep, tiered cascade falls are fed year-round by both springs and melting ice fields off Mount Hood.

6. Mirror Lake ☺ ⚲ ⚙ 🐾 ☀

- Northwest Forest Pass
- Easy
- 4.4 miles round trip out and back
- 640 feet elevation gain
- 2–2.5 hours

Mirror Lake trailhead is just off Highway 26 and close enough to Portland for city hikers to come after work. It's a peaceful lake with a heavenly reflection of Mount Hood, an image gracing postcards and flooding social media, but it tends to be crowded. If you come in the off-season, midweek, you'll have a better experience. The crowds thin out after Mirror Lake, if you choose to carry on up the Tom, Dick, and Harry Mountain Trail for another couple of miles. The views from the top of the mountain are breathtaking.

7. Trillium Lake Loop ☺ ⚲ ⚙ 🍂 🐾

- Day-use fee (pay at the kiosk in the parking lot)
- Easy
- 1.9-mile loop
- 10 feet elevation gain
- 1 hour

Enjoy a leisurely stroll around the lake, where you can fish, swim, and play in the cold water. There's a wheelchair-accessible fishing pier and a boat launch (nonmotorized only). It's a wonderful way to while away a summer afternoon, with a large campground on-site to hang your hammock.

8. Zigzag Overlook ☺ ⚲ ⚙ ☀

- Wilderness permit*
- Easy to moderate
- 4.4 miles round trip out and back
- 820 feet elevation gain
- 3 hours

This hike will introduce you to Mount Hood's sunny southside meadows, requiring little effort as it wanders through small valleys crisscrossed with snowmelt streams. In the summer the trail is lined with wildflowers. Treat yourself at the end of the hike with lunch at the Timberline Lodge.

Purchase a wilderness permit at the trailhead kiosk.

9. Mountaineer Trail Loop ⚱ ⚙ ✷

- No pass required
- Moderate
- 2.7 miles round trip out and back
- 1,065 feet elevation gain
- 2.5 hours

This high-elevation hike (up to 7,000 feet) is on the flanks of Mount Hood and takes you to Silcox Hut, built in 1939 as the upper terminal of the original Magic Mile chairlift. It's been restored and is used today as an overnight group rental. You can always skip the second part of the loop and take the Magic Mile chairlift back down for a shorter hike.

10. Umbrella Falls/Sahale Falls Loop ☺ ⚱ ⚙ 🌿 🐾 〰

- Wilderness permit self-issued at trailhead
- Easy to moderate
- 5 miles round trip out and back
- 840 feet elevation gain
- 3 hours

The scenic trail is near Hood River Meadows, where wildflowers blaze the way to these lovely waterfalls. Umbrella is a veiled horsetail falls, Sahale a tiered horsetail. The trail is outside the Mount Hood Wilderness area, and you could be sharing with mountain bikers. Watch for frogs in the many creeks you'll cross. *mounthoodinfo.com*

MULTIDAY BACKPACKING

11. Salmon River ☺ 🌿 🐾 ✷

- Northwest Forest Pass, wilderness permit self-issued at trailhead
- Moderate
- 7.8 miles round trip out and back
- 950 feet elevation gain
- 4 hours

This is one of my favorite hikes along the pristine Salmon River, showcasing its moody changes and ever-present river song. There are multiple excellent campsites along the way, beginning a short distance up the trail, but you'll need luck or timing on your side—this area is a popular backpacking getaway. The canyon viewpoint at around 4 miles offers a wide vista of the Salmon-Huckleberry Wilderness area; take a short night hike there for perfect stargazing. This is the hike's turnaround point. Note that the severely underfunded USFS is considering closing the Salmon River corridor to all backcountry camping because of needless tree and plant damage and the enormous amount of garbage, human waste, and toilet paper left behind. If you want continued overnight access to this majestic river, leave no trace! Pack everything out and stay on the established trail.

12. Burnt Lake ✿ ✂ 🐾 👣 ♨

- Wilderness permit self-issued at trailhead (May 15 to October 15)
- Easy to moderate
- 6.6 miles round trip out and back
- 1,420 feet elevation gain
- 4 hours

The hike begins as a gentle walk and then throws a curveball with a steep ascent at the last mile. Carry on for rich views, a pretty lake, and some fishing (like tenkara; see page 109) if desired. The trail circles the lake and there are many places to camp here, but keep in mind there are also designated day-use sites. The sites with numbered posts are for camping and the lettered are for day-use only. For a thigh-burning hike in the morning, head up the trail to East Zigzag Mountain for more knockout vistas, then return to camp for a refreshing dip in the lake.

13. Meditation Point ☺ ✂ 🐾 👣

- Parking fee (pay at the West Shore day-use parking lot)
- Easy
- 2 miles round trip out and back
- Negligible elevation gain
- 1 hour

This backpacking hike is everything a family with young children could hope for: the way out is flat and less than 1 mile long, there's a lake to splash in, and the setting is, well, meditatively beautiful. The path to Meditation Point from the West Shore day-use parking lot is gentle enough that you could pull a wagon full of gear and a toddler to the campsite. There's fishing and crawdads and escape from the crowds at this popular lake, but only 4 primitive first-come, first-served sites, and no potable water. Bring a filter for the lake water or bring water from home. *oregonsbestcamping.com/mt_hood/meditation_point.html*

14. Lower Twin Lake ☺ ✿ ✂ 🐾

- Northwest Forest Pass
- Easy to moderate
- 4.2 miles round trip out and back
- 660 feet elevation gain
- 2 hours

This hike is popular year-round—in summer with day hikers and backpackers, and in winter with snowshoers and skiers. Those who crave solitude won't find it here, but it's an appealing campout especially if you can make it midweek in the early fall. Follow the lakeside trail to find a campsite, and in the morning explore Upper Twin Lake.

15. Elk Meadows ✿ ✂ 🦌 🐾 ✨ ≋

- Northwest Forest Pass, wilderness permit self-issued at trailhead
- Moderate
- 5.8 miles round trip out and back
- 1,200 feet elevation gain
- 4 hours

Elk Meadows, a wildflower feast for the eyes, is considered one of the most stunning alpine meadows in the Mount Hood area. Once you make camp, there are many trail options for further exploration in the coming days, with lots of bang for your hiking buck, including a loop trail that circles the meadow and a small spur trail that goes to its center. Take it. You'll feel like Dorothy in the land of Oz. There are many other trail options on the return if desired.

EXPLORE MORE ADVENTURES

Fly Down an Alpine Slide

This 0.5-mile slide down the mountain at Skibowl is crazy fun. Ride the chairlift up, and hurtle down on a rolling curvy track built of slippery fiberglass. A plastic sled sends you at speeds of up to 35 mph down S curves and banked turns. You do have brakes to control the speed, however. *skibowl.com*

Mountain Bike the Timberline to Town Trail

This 18-mile intermediate track, affectionately called the T2T, is hands-down the most popular ride in the Mount Hood area. Take a bus shuttle with your bike from the village of Rhododendron up to Timberline Lodge and cycle down a single track back to your car. The mixed trail starts out on pumice-like sand and rocky terrain but gives way to a smoother track on the Pioneer Bridle Trail. As an added bonus there are plenty of places to stop for lunch along the way. The bus fills fast on weekends; you'll have to arrive early. For more chairlift-assisted trails, check out the Timberline Bike Park. *singletracks.com*

Ski a Glacier in Summer

Timberline offers the longest ski season in North America on Palmer Glacier, one of the 12 glaciers that cloak Mount Hood. In the summer the upper half of the glacier is divided between general public use and ski and snowboard camps. The lift closes from late summer until the first snows of autumn; check the Timberline website for conditions before you go. *timberlinelodge.com*

Take a Rock-Climbing Tour on French's Dome

Spend the day on a geological wonder. Mt. Hood Outfitters will take climbers, whether beginners or more seasoned, on a rock-climbing tour of French's Dome—a basalt remnant of an old volcano neck core left after the softer outer rock eroded away. There are a variety of routes on this crag to fit all levels, with excellent views of Mount Hood from the top and a fun rappel back down. *mthoodoutfitters.com*

Night Hike: Watch the Full Moon Rise from Silcox Hut

The hike up to Silcox Hut is a wide-open trail, 1 mile long with 1,000 feet of elevation gain, but you'll be heading up in dusk's ambient light and hiking back down under a full moon. Bring headlamps, an extra layer to keep warm, a camp chair, and plenty of water. The beauty of a rising full moon in the mountains awaits. *oregonhikers.org*

Season of Snow

When driving to Mount Hood in winter, you must carry chains if you don't have studded tires. Check road conditions and the weather forecast before leaving.

SNOWSHOE TRAILS

Crosstown Trail

This trail is the longest and one of the most versatile in the Government Camp network of winter trails, with many loops and options available to shorten it. Pick your skill level—several junctions give you choices from beginner to intermediate. *fs.usda.gov*

Enid Lake Loop

Another trail off the Government Camp network, this one is rated moderate as it wends up and down the hills around Enid Lake. It's a 2-mile loop; take your time negotiating the trickier sections. *fs.usda.gov*

Trillium Lake Loop

The 3.6-mile loop around Trillium Lake offers stunning views of Mount Hood on a clear day without a lot of elevation gain. There's also a sledding area to add to the fun. *alltrails.com*

Frog Lake

The Frog Lake Trail is a wide and flat trail excellent for beginners, without much elevation gain. The parking lot at the Frog Lake Sno-Park can be congested with snowmobilers, but there are plenty of other trails for the vroom crowd. *fs.usda.gov*

White River West Sno-Park

This Sno-Park offers something for all ability levels. The best part is the wide-open vista and Mount Hood so close you can almost reach out and touch it. Go past the crowds of sledders and continue up—you can blaze your own trail and not get lost. The lot fills fast on weekends, so plan to get there early. Sno-Park pass required.

MOUNT HOOD NATIONAL FOREST, OREGON

CROSS-COUNTRY SKI TRAILS

Teacup Lake

There are over 12 miles of groomed trails with a warming hut. Snowshoes are prohibited, and there's an on-site donation request to contribute toward grooming costs. *teacupnordic.org*

Mt. Hood Meadows Nordic Center

The center is generally open on weekends and holidays throughout the winter and has 10 miles of groomed skate-skiing and cross country skiing track through wooded trails and meadows. Rentals available; snowshoes prohibited. *skihood.com*

Cooper Spur Nordic Center

Take your pick: there are separate trails for snowshoers and 4 miles of cross-country ski trails groomed for both skate-skiing and traditional cross-country skiing. Rentals available.

DOWNHILL SKI AND SNOWBOARD TRIPS

Mt. Hood Meadows

This is one of the largest ski resorts in Oregon, with 2,150 acres, 11 chairlifts (including 6 high-speed quads), and a thigh-burning 3-mile run, but bigger isn't always better—it's on the southeast side of the mountain and it often gets slammed with storms. Check the weather forecast before leaving.

Mt. Hood Skibowl

It's steep and cheap, as locals say, with more black diamond runs than the other resorts. This is a local's mountain with shorter lift lines, especially at the upper bowl. The fantastic night skiing here is one of the largest in the country, with 34 well-lit runs available 7 days a week.

Timberline

The lodge alone makes skiing here an iconic experience, with a classic après-ski crowd sipping cocktails after hitting the slopes. It's the only true ski-in ski-out place on the mountain, a good getaway. The slopes offer mellower ski runs and an imposing freestyle terrain park for snowboarders. The 6,000-foot elevation at the base means more snow here, and powder is all but guaranteed at the top at 8,540 feet.

Summit Ski Area

It's old, small, and a bit creaky, but that's to be expected at the oldest continuously operating ski resort in the Pacific Northwest. It's basically a beginner's bunny hill; visit the fun tubing area when you are finished with the three ski trails.

Cooper Spur

Cooper Spur is on the quieter northeast side of Mount Hood and the ski area is small and inexpensive, but what it lacks in vertical, it makes up for with a sprawl of nearby cabins and a small funky lodge to stay at.

SLEDDING AND TUBING

Mt. Hood Skibowl Cosmic Tubing

Visit during the day for regular tubing on well-groomed slopes (and a dedicated conveyor ride to the top), but if that's too tame, on weekend nights there's Cosmic Tubing: tubing and a light show set to blasting music. Crazy fun for all! Tickets must be bought online. *skibowl.com/tubing /cosmic-tubing.html*

Snow Bunny Play Area

Summit Ski Area runs this weekends-only tubing adventure on dedicated runs that are long and clear and offer a variety of pitches to slide down. No personal sledding devices are permitted, but you can rent their old-fashioned tire tubes. You have to walk your tube back up, but your pass is good all day and this is tubing at its bygone best.

White River West Sno-Park

This is a winter recreation area for all ages with many activities, but sledding is hugely popular. There's over a half mile of sledding from the Sno-Park with a wide variety of terrain that even the teenagers among us will love. The view of Mount Hood makes a cinema-worthy backdrop. Sno-Park pass required.

Trillium Lake

At the end of the Trillium Lake parking lot, find it all here for free—gentle slopes for the timid and steep chutes for the confident. Bring your own sleds and tubes and plan on spending a wild and wonderful afternoon.

EXPLORE MORE ADVENTURES

Watch the Frog Lake Dogsled Race

This 2-day event held in January is a blast. The Cascade Sled Dog Club sponsors the race and it includes skijor races (dogs pulling a skier) and bikejor races (dogs pulling a fat bike) as well as the traditional sprints and distance races. The club also offers a demo for kids on Saturday: they can stand on the runners while a racing dog pulls them a short distance. Registration is necessary—there are usually more kids than available sleds and dogs. Wear lots of layers and bring heavy blankets, camp chairs, and a picnic. *cascadesleddogclub.com/froglake*

Snowshoe to an Icefall

Tamanawas Falls is a beauty in summer, but in winter it is a magnificent scene of snow and ice. The gentle 2-mile trail is easy enough for beginners, but that also means it draws a lot of traffic on weekends. Plan accordingly and shoot for midweek if you can. *theoutbound.com*

Cut Your Own Christmas Tree

Start the holiday season by cutting your own Christmas tree in a select area of the national forest and hauling it home. You'll be contributing to good forest management practices at the same time. Here are the rules:

- Buy a permit.
- There must be a tree of similar size within 8 feet of the one you cut.

- Each permit allows you to cut one tree up to 15 feet high, leaving a stump height of no more than 6 inches.
- Cutting the top off of a standing tree is prohibited.
- Do not cut trees within a wilderness, research natural area, campground, or within 300 feet of streams or lakes.
- Use a handsaw.
- When your tree is cut, attach the permit to the tree.

Be safe! It's easy to get lost when you are laser-focused on finding the right tree. Carry the 10 Essentials, emergency supplies, and extra warm clothing. At the end of the searching and sawing and hauling, reward yourself with a stop at Joe's Donuts in Sandy. *mthoodterritory.com*

Stay at the Tilly Jane Hut by Snowshoe

This large communal A-frame cabin sleeps 20 and is super popular during the winter for its backcountry snowshoeing, boarding, and skiing opportunities. It has a funky *Portlandia* vibe as day trippers move in and out to mingle with those who reserved an overnight visit. Reaching Tilly takes a hefty, sometimes steep, 2.7-mile snowshoe hike with a loaded pack carrying everything you'll need for an overnight. Heat is from a woodstove; there's no electricity or running water, but at night people play cards and fellow foodies share their best backcountry cocktail recipes. What more could you ask? *recreation.gov*

SISTERS PEAKS, OREGON

Deschutes National Forest, Oregon

Bend and Sisters Area

Deschutes National Forest encompasses a young and complex volcanic region on the eastern flank of Oregon's Cascade Range. Cinder cones and large composite volcanoes eroded by glaciers are scattered across the landscape. At 1.6 million acres, the national forest is an immense and diverse region with a wide variety of ecosystems and a long history of human habitation. Before the Oregon Territory was formed, before the communities of Bend and Sisters were established, Indigenous peoples flourished in the region for thousands of years, living from the land and the rivers. This is the ancestral home of the Tenino people, today represented with other tribes by the Confederated Tribes of Warm Springs, and they continue to shape and protect the land with the belief that the environment and the people who live there cannot be separated, a tenet for all outdoor enthusiasts. The Native name for the Three Sisters Mountains is Klah Klahnee, or "Three Points."

Deschutes National Forest is vast and includes five wilderness areas with endless recreation opportunities. To protect and stabilize the fragile ecosystems of the wilderness areas, all hikes within their boundaries have a strict quota of hikers for both overnight and day hiking between the Friday of Memorial Day weekend and the last Friday of September, governed by permit. The permits need to be purchased in advance (*recreation.gov /ticket/facility/300009*); there are only a few available at the trailheads during the 4 months of the limited entry, and it is enforced. Visit one of the following ranger stations (find them all at *fs.usda.gov*) for maps, weather forecast, permits (including backcountry), and local information:

- Bend–Fort Rock Ranger District Office
- Sisters Ranger District Office
- Cascade Lakes Welcome Station

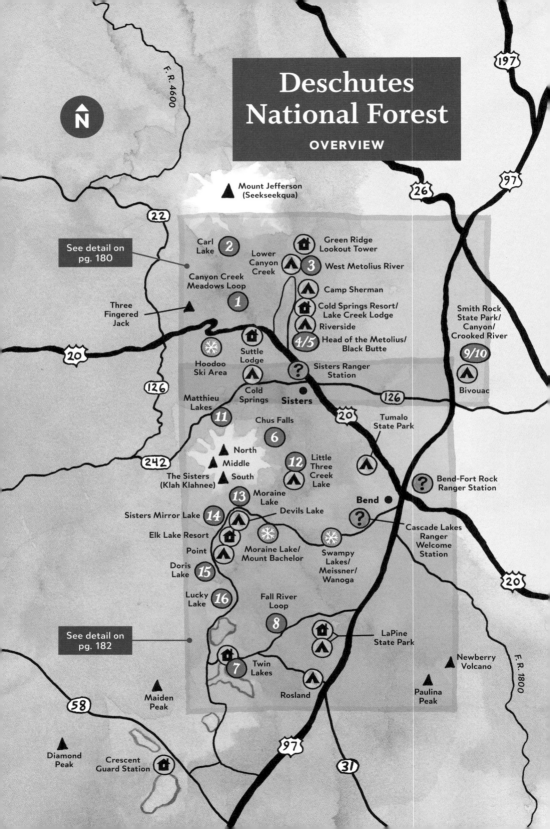

Deschutes
National Forest
OVERVIEW

N

F. R. 4600

197

97

26

22

Mount Jefferson
(Seekseekqua)

Carl Lake — 2

See detail on pg. 180

Canyon Creek Meadows Loop — 1

Lower Canyon Creek

Green Ridge Lookout Tower

3 — West Metolius River

Three Fingered Jack

Camp Sherman

Cold Springs Resort/ Lake Creek Lodge

Riverside

4/5 — Head of the Metolius/ Black Butte

Smith Rock State Park/ Canyon/ Crooked River

9/10

Hoodoo Ski Area

Suttle Lodge

Sisters Ranger Station

Bivouac

20

126

Cold Springs

Sisters

126

Matthieu Lakes — 11

Chus Falls

6

Tumalo State Park

242

North

Middle

The Sisters (Klah Klahnee)

South

12 — Little Three Creek Lake

20

Bend-Fort Rock Ranger Station

13 — Moraine Lake

Bend

Sisters Mirror Lake — 14

Devils Lake

Elk Lake Resort

Point

Moraine Lake/ Mount Bachelor

Swampy Lakes/ Meissner/ Wanoga

Cascade Lakes Ranger Welcome Station

Doris Lake — 15

Lucky Lake — 16

Fall River Loop

20

See detail on pg. 182

8

LaPine State Park

Newberry Volcano

7 — Twin Lakes

Rosland

Paulina Peak

F. R. 1800

58

Maiden Peak

Diamond Peak

Crescent Guard Station

97

31

Get Away

CAMPGROUNDS ▲

Riverside

There are many campgrounds along the scenic Metolius River, one of the clearest and coldest rivers in Oregon, but Riverside is the more remote and quiet choice for campers. The 16 spacious and grassy walk-in sites are reservable and not far from the unique headwaters of the Metolius River, which surge from an underground spring. Pets allowed on leashes; closed in winter.

Camp Sherman ♿

Bike, hike, fly-fish—pick your passion—from the campground of Camp Sherman. A few minutes away is the charming town of Camp Sherman, with a general store and hot showers. There are 15 reservable sites; pets allowed on leashes; open year-round.

Lower Canyon Creek

Located at the confluence of Canyon Creek and the fabled Upper Metolius River, this special campground is spacious and crowd-free with only 7 reservable sites. The trailhead to Wizard Falls Fish Hatchery is located here. There is no potable water, so you'll have to bring your own; pets allowed on leashes; closed in winter.

Tumalo State Park ♿

Set along the Deschutes River, this is one of the closest campgrounds to Bend and it's an excellent base camp for exploring everything the Bend/Sisters area has to offer. There are 77 reservable campsites (54 tent-only) and 7 yurts offered for a step up in comfort. Hot showers, a playground, and dedicated hiker/biker campsites (first come, first served) make this a user-friendly place in all seasons. Pets allowed on leashes.

Three Creek Lake

The campground is one of three around Three Creek Lake, with splendid hiking options nearby and plenty of water activities to keep everyone happy. Canoe and paddleboard rentals are available at nearby Three

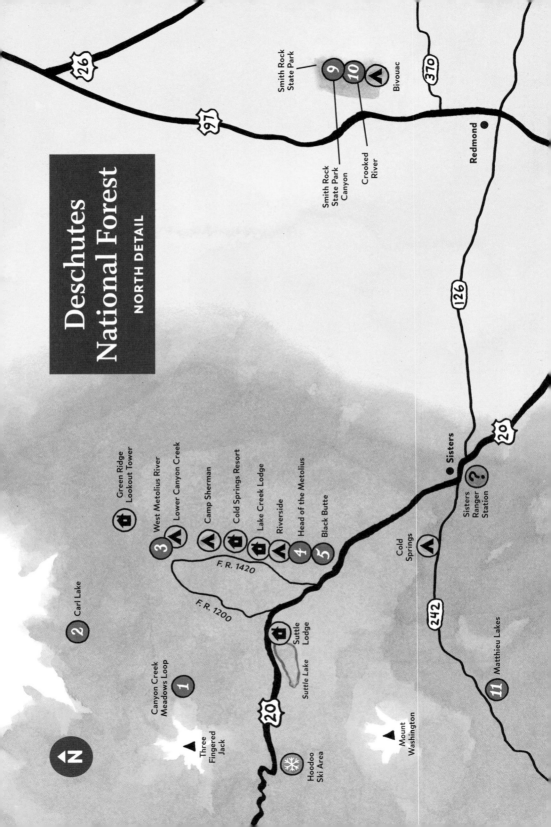

Deschutes
National Forest
NORTH DETAIL

Creek Lake Store. Most of the 11 sites are reservable, with a few set aside for first come, first served. No potable water; pets allowed on leashes; closed in winter.

Devils Lake

This small walk-in tent-only campground is the gateway to Three Sisters Wilderness hiking. It's situated along the clear waters of Devils Lake, which is spring fed and has good fishing. There is no fee to camp here, but you will need a recreation pass (Northwest Forest Pass or American the Beautiful Pass) for your car. There are 11 sites (all first come, first served) and no potable water, so bring your own or treat the lake water with a filtration system. Pets allowed on leashes; closed in winter.

Point

This small, shady campground is on the shore of Elk Lake, which has a sandy beach, a boat ramp, and a host of water activities, including sailing and windsurfing. Most of the 9 sites are reservable, but some are available first come, first served. Pets allowed on leashes; closed in winter.

LaPine State Park ♿

There is legendary fly-fishing near this campground along the Deschutes River, as well as multiple mountain biking trails and hiking opportunities. It's large, with 82 reservable campsites and many amenities, like hot showers and electric hookups. Pets allowed on leashes; open year-round.

Rosland

Explore the Little Deschutes River from Rosland by bird-watching, fishing, hiking, or taking a tube float down the river from Leona Park. First come, first served; pets allowed on leashes; closed in winter.

Cold Springs ♿

This sweet campground is located just west of the town of Sisters and is a popular place to camp during the Sisters Rodeo in early June. Bird lovers may sight pygmy nuthatches or forest owls along Trout Creek, and the amazing Dee Wright Observatory (see page 195) is only 11 miles down the road. There are 22 reservable campsites; pets allowed on leashes; closed in winter.

Deschutes National Forest
SOUTH DETAIL

N

126

242

20

US 97

US 20

11 Matthieu Lakes

Cold Springs

Sisters

Sisters Ranger Station

Bend–Fort Rock Ranger District

▲ North Sister

▲ Middle Sister

6 Chus Falls

Tumalo State Park

▲ South Sister

▲ Broken Top

12 Little Three Creek Lake

Three Creek Lake

Bend

13 Moraine Lake

Sisters Mirror Lake

14

Devils Lake

Mount Bachelor Ski Resort

Moraine Lake

Cascade Lakes Ranger/Welcome Station

Swampy Lakes/ Meissner Sno-Parks

Elk Lake Resort

Point

Mount Bachelor

Wanoga Snow Play Area

15 Doris Lake

Lava Lands Visitor Center

16 Lucky Lake

F. R. 4500

Sunriver

F. R. 4000

Craine Prairie Reservoir

F. R. 4200

Fall River Loop

8

LaPine State Park

Newberry Volcano ▲

Twin Lakes Resort

Twin Lakes Loop

F. R. 4300

7

Wickiup Reservoir

Rosland

97

LaPine

Paulina Peak ▲

Bivouac

Bivouac—or the Bivy, as it is affectionately known—is the headquarters for rock climbers at Smith Rock. Perched on a rim-rock plateau with great views of the park's 500-foot rock faces, the Bivy offers showers and an electronics charging station. Walk-in tent camping only, with no campers or RVs allowed. First come, first served; pets allowed on leashes; open year-round.

CABINS AND LODGES ⌂

The Suttle Lodge ♿

This hip lodge has a decidedly *Portlandia* flair. There are 11 rooms in the lodge and 16 cabins that range from fully equipped deluxe to rustic with few amenities. A nice feature of the lodge is the community spaces— clusters of outdoor seating that encourage groups to mingle. It's also a foodie destination for folks who want scrumptious on-site options, including handcrafted cocktails and themed dinner parties created by celebrated chefs.

Cold Springs Resort

Cold Springs Resort is on the shore of the Metolius River and offers excellent trout fishing, as well as nearby hiking and mountain biking for all levels. These pleasant cabin rentals are moderately priced for the Bend area, with several of them pet friendly. RV sites are also available on the property.

Lake Creek Lodge ♿

This family-friendly lodge has 21 fully equipped cabins, a fishing pond on-site, a swimming pool, and a restaurant for the days you don't want to cook.

Green Ridge Lookout

This active lookout is run by the US Forest Service (USFS) and used most of the summer, but there are windows from early May through June and mid-September through mid-November for the lucky few who can secure a reservation. The views are breathtaking, it's easily accessed without a grueling climb, and it's a bird-watcher's dream. Wizard Falls Fish Hatchery is located just below Green Ridge, where they feed the eagles every morning. Bring all the water you'll need, along with bedding. *recreation.gov*

Elk Lake Resort ♿

In summer the resort offers a marina with boat, paddleboard, and kayak rentals, and nearby hiking and biking trails. Accommodations include regular cabins, glamping tents and cabins, and a campground. It's open in winter and is a busy hub for snow activities, including fat tire biking, snowshoeing, and snowmobile rentals. In winter, a snowcat shuttle to the resort is offered with prior arrangement.

LaPine State Park Cabins ♿

Along with the campground and the yurts here, there are 5 rustic and 5 deluxe cabins to rent at LaPine State Park, where there are snowshoe and cross-country ski trails in winter and plenty of family-friendly activities year-round.

Twin Lakes Resort ♿

Located on the shores of South Twin Lake, this is another family-friendly option with full amenities, including a country store, a restaurant, and boat rentals. Find a variety of moderately priced accommodations, from cabin rentals to campsites and sites with full RV hookups.

Crescent Guard Station

Guard stations were originally built in the 1920s and 1930s as outposts for USFS rangers to manage huge tracts of land; today you can rent Crescent Guard Station, set above the shore of Crescent Lake, which has sandy beaches and aquamarine water. You'll have to be quick and lucky to get a reservation. It's a handsome cabin with more amenities than a typical lookout, including a bathroom, running water, and heat. No pets allowed inside; closed in winter. *fs.usda.gov*

Season of Green

DAY HIKES

1. Canyon Creek Meadows ✿ 🐾 ☀ ♨

- Northwest Forest Pass; day-use permit self-issued at trailhead in off-season; wilderness permit required in summer*
- Easy
- 4.5 miles
- 400 feet elevation gain
- 2.5 hours

This popular hike takes you to a stunning wildflower meadow at the base of Three Fingered Jack, which looms in craggy splendor over the colorful show. The best time to visit the meadows is in July. Stay on the trails! This delicate habitat has been damaged by careless hikers in the past. Picnic in the trees or at Wasco Lake, a 0.7-mile detour, where you can swim. *oregonhikers.org*

2. Carl Lake ✿ 🌿 🍁 🐾

- Day-use permit self-issued at trailhead in off-season; wilderness permit required in summer*
- Moderate
- 10 miles round trip out and back
- 1,000 feet elevation gain
- 5–6 hours

Located in Mount Jefferson Wilderness, Carl Lake is an alpine oasis that you can camp at for a relatively easy overnight trip (you'll need a backcountry permit). Take the short side trail to Cabot Lake on the way; it's worth a stop and a dip on hot summer days. *oregonhikers.org*

From the Friday of Memorial Day weekend through September, a limited entry day-use permit is required; purchase in advance from recreation.gov /ticket/facility/300009.

3. West Metolius River 🧍 ⚙ 🍂 🐾

- No pass required
- Easy
- 5.5 miles round trip out and back to Wizard Falls hatchery

- 100 feet elevation gain
- 2.5 hours

The Metolius is a magical river. Warm Springs Natives named it *mitula*, or "white salmon," for the chinook salmon that were once abundant here. With this hike you'll get a fascinating glimpse of the fish life cycle at the Wizard Falls Fish Hatchery. The West Metolius River Trail begins at Lower Canyon Creek Campground, and the turnaround point is 2.2 miles in, at the hatchery. Although there are no guided tours, you can explore the raceways, where several species of salmon and trout fingerlings are raised; informative panels explain the process. *fs.usda.gov*

4. Head of the Metolius 🧍 🍂 🐾 ⭐ 🚴

- No pass required
- Easy
- 0.5 mile round trip out and back

- 20 feet elevation gain
- 40 minutes

The Metolius River is geologically unique. Most rivers begin with snowmelt from mountains that gather into streams, joining as they flow to create bigger streams that eventually merge to create a river, but the Metolius headwaters gush from huge springs at the foot of Black Butte. Geologists believe the springs originate deep in the west Cascades and travel a fault line to the butte. The springs pour out 50,000 gallons per minute and *immediately* create a large and commanding river. Take a short hike to see the phenomenon on this easy trail. *fs.usda.gov*

5. Black Butte 🐾 ⭐

- Northwest Forest Pass
- Moderate
- 4 miles round trip out and back

- 1,500 feet elevation gain
- 2.5–3 hours

The hike up this stratovolcano is demanding, with a steady ascent, but the payoff is huge: it offers one of the most commanding views of the Oregon Cascades you'll find. The lookout tower at the summit has a mountain identification panel to guide your eye through the grandeur of this range.

The trail can be hot and dusty in the summer, so bring sunscreen and plenty of water. *fs.usda.gov*

6. Chus Falls 🍁 ⚙️ 🐾 🏊

- Day-use permit self-issued at trailhead in off-season; wilderness permit required in summer*
- Easy
- 5.7 miles round trip out and back
- 300 feet elevation gain
- 3–4 hours

The trail to Chus Falls follows the pretty Whychus Creek, with plenty of views of South Sister and falling cascades along the way. Chus is a robust veiled plunge waterfall, 75 feet wide with a 67-foot drop, and the sheer volume of water exudes thunderous power. In late June the wildflowers add to the bucolic landscape. *fs.usda.gov*

7. Twin Lakes Loop 🏕️ ⚙️ 🍁 🐾

- Parking fee (pay at Twin Lakes Resort)
- Easy
- 4.5 miles round trip
- 350 feet elevation gain
- 2.5 hours

This trail is a great one for little hikers, with ice cream at Twin Lakes Resort as a reward at the end. Too hot to hike? Swim, rent a kayak, or simply pack a picnic and choose the nearest beach. *alltrails.com*

8. Fall River Loop 🏕️ 🍁 🐾 🏊

- Northwest Forest Pass
- Easy
- 1.9-mile loop
- 50 feet elevation gain
- 1.5 hours

Take your fly rod on this short hike to the headwaters of the Fall River, or enjoy watching for beavers and birds as the river flows lazily beside you. Take your time; this is an excellent hike for bringing a sketch pad and a picnic and sitting beside the river. *visitbend.com*

*From the Friday of Memorial Day weekend through September, a limited entry day-use permit is required; purchase in advance from recreation.gov /ticket/facility/300009.

METOLIUS RIVER, OREGON

9. Smith Rock State Park Canyon 👤 🦅 🐾

- Day-use fee (pay at the parking lot)
- Moderate

- 3.3 miles round trip out and back
- 440 feet elevation gain
- 1.5 hours

Smith Rock State Park is a rock climber's paradise, with a stunning landscape of volcanic ash spires that rise from the high desert floor in red-hued splendor. While on the canyon trail, watch for wildlife, an abundance of birds, and rock climbers as they pick their way up the epic towers. Bring sunscreen and plenty of water, and try to hit the trail early in the morning to avoid crowds. *alltrails.com*

10. Crooked River Trail 👤 ⚙ 🦅 🐾

- Day-use fee (pay at the parking lot)
- Easy

- 4.4 miles round trip out and back
- 322 feet elevation gain
- 3 hours

The pros of this gorgeous trail in Smith Rock State Park: it follows the Crooked River, there is bountiful wildlife, and you'll find plenty of riverside places to pull off and enjoy lunch. The cons: it can be crowded and blazing hot and dusty in July and August. Don't let that stop you; this hike is a gem. Start early in the morning and salute the sunrise. *alltrails.com*

MULTIDAY BACKPACKING

11. Matthieu Lakes ⚙ 🐾

- Northwest Forest Pass, self-issued wilderness permit at trailhead
- Moderate

- 6-mile loop
- 800 feet elevation gain
- 3.5 hours

This popular hike to the two Matthieu Lakes will give you a taste of the Pacific Crest Trail and an enjoyable overnight backpacking trip. The trail can be dusty in summer, but you arrive to knockout views of the Three Sisters (Klah Klanee), Mount Jefferson (Seekseekqua), and Three Fingered Jack. North Matthieu Lake is warmer than the south lake and makes a great place to cool off after a hot hike. *alltrails.com*

12. Little Three Creek Lake 🧍 ⚙ 🍁 🐾

- Northwest Forest Pass; permit self-issued at trailhead in off-season; wilderness permit required in summer*
- Easy
- 2.7 miles round trip out and back
- 230 feet elevation gain
- 1.5 hours

There are two lakes on this beginner-friendly backpack trip: Three Creek Lake and Little Three Creek Lake, both gin clear and lying in a glacial cirque at the base of Tam McArthur Rim. Your destination is Little Three Creek Lake, where there are good campsites along the shore to pitch your tent. Bring a fly rod for fishing at dusk. *alltrails.com*

13. Moraine Lake ⚙ 🐾 ⭐ ♨

- Northwest Forest Pass; permit self-issued at trailhead in off-season; wilderness permit required in summer*
- Moderate
- 4.6 miles round trip out and back
- 1,500 feet elevation gain
- 2.5–3 hours

If you hike this trail in the summer, plan to arrive early—parking can be hard to find after 10:00 a.m. However, most hikers are heading to Green Lakes, and you will be peeling off to Moraine Lake, which offers more solitude. It lies at the foot of the Lewis Glacier; there are 22 designated primitive campsites and several options for further adventures, including hiking to Green Lakes and summiting South Sister. To protect the fragile plant life, you must set up within 15 feet of the campsite markers. Exceptional star gazing at night! *fs.usda.gov*

From the Friday of Memorial Day weekend through September, a limited entry day-use permit is required; purchase in advance from recreation.gov /ticket/facility/300009.

14. Sisters Mirror Lake ⚙ 🦋 🐾

- Northwest Forest Pass; permit self-issued at trailhead in off-season; wilderness permit required in summer*
- Moderate
- 9.7 miles round trip out and back
- 665 feet elevation gain
- 5 hours

On this hike into the Three Sisters Wilderness, you will see lava flows, forests of mountain hemlock, meadows, and creeks. There are more than a dozen small alpine lakes in the Sisters Mirror Lake area, many with campsites along their shores. Mosquitoes are a problem in early and mid-summer, so bring bug spray. *alltrails.com*

15. Doris Lake 🦋 🐾

- Northwest Forest Pass; permit self-issued at trailhead in off-season; wilderness permit required in summer*
- Easy
- 5 miles round trip out and back
- 400 feet elevation gain
- 2.5 hours

Doris Lake, along the Six Lakes Trail, has pebbly beaches, crystal-clear water, and plenty of trees for hanging a hammock. From your base camp at Doris Lake, hike farther up the trail the next morning to Mink and Cliff Lakes, and hook up with the Pacific Crest Trail. Be prepared for mosquitoes in spring through midsummer. *alltrails.com*

16. Lucky Lake ⚙ 🦋 🐾

- Northwest Forest Pass; permit self-issued at trailhead in off-season; wilderness permit required in summer*
- Easy
- 3-mile loop
- 400 feet elevation gain
- 1.5 hours

The Lucky Lake trailhead is a bit farther from Bend than other hikes featured here, but there's more solitude and a cool lake with several beach access points for swimming on a hot summer day. The hike in is an easy mile to several unmarked camping spots around the shore for backpackers, perfect for beginners and little hikers. The loop includes hiking around the lake. *alltrails.com*

EXPLORE MORE ADVENTURES

Cycle the Sisters to Smith Rock Scenic Bikeway

Oregon is the first state to map dedicated scenic routes for bikes. The 15 routes feature gorgeous scenery, little traffic, and local history on some of Oregon's best side roads. Cycle the moderate-rated Sisters to Smith Rock and experience one of them. After downloading the map, begin early with breakfast at one of the local cafes in Sisters, where the bikeway starts. There's a public park at each end of the route, where you can park a vehicle and shuttle back. This 37-mile cycle (one way) will take you over rolling hills and alongside rivers, offer stunning views of the Cascades, and deliver you to the arresting volcanic spires of Smith Rock. Bonus: there's only 710 feet of elevation gain, but consider renting an electric bike if the mileage feels like a stretch. *visitbend.com*

Learn to Rock Climb at Smith Rock

Smith Rock Climbing holds a multiday course tailored to your experience—whether you're a beginner or simply want to enhance your skills. Climbing several days in a row is the best way to jump-start this exhilarating sport, and Smith Rock is an iconic place to learn. *smithrockclimbing.com*

Fly-Fish a 12-Hole Course

The Bend/Sisters region is famous for its outstanding fly-fishing, with pristine river systems, lakes, and creeks in a spectacular landscape. Practice your skills on the Old Mill District Fly Casting Course in Bend, a unique 12-hole course open to the public for free. Think of golf with a fly rod. The casting course guide brochure includes a map, casting tips, and a scorecard. Many local fly-fishing shops offer lessons using the course, so you can increase your casting skills before taking advantage of fly-fishing paradise in the Deschutes National Forest. *oldmilldistrict.com*

Bike and Brew Suttle Lake Loop

The scenic 3.6-mile mountain bike trail around Suttle Lake sticks to the shore and is relatively flat, gaining less than 500 feet in elevation. But a few rocks and stumps keep things interesting. You'll encounter hikers. End at the Suttle Lodge for an ice-cold beer and a classic poutine lunch. *alltrails.com*

Tube the Deschutes

Float a section of the Deschutes River on a blazing summer day and let the world carry on without you. Start at Riverbend Park in Bend and float for about 45 minutes to the Colorado Avenue bridge. Stay in your raft to ride the waves through Bend Whitewater Park, or exit the river and walk through the tunnel to a put-in that avoids the rapids. Continue to drift on to the takeout at lovely Drake Park. The float takes around 2 long and lazy hours. *bendparksandrec.org*

Test Your Whitewater Skills at Bend Whitewater Park

Bend Whitewater Park is in the heart of Bend on the Deschutes River. It was created when an aging and hazardous dam was modified at the Colorado Avenue bridge and the river was divided into three channels—one for floaters, one for wildlife, and one, the middle channel, for whitewater enthusiasts. The fun starts in this channel, which is ingeniously engineered with pneumatic bladders that make four standing waves of varying difficulty. Whether you're a novice paddler or expert surfer, you can choose the wave intensity to practice your skills at this water playground—or simply watch the fun.

See the Great Western Toadlet Migration

Little Three Creek Lake is a toadlet mecca. Each year between June and July, adult native western toads migrate from the nearby forests to the waterways of central Oregon's ponds and lakes to breed. A female toad can lay over 15,000 eggs, and you can see the eggs, like skeins of black pearls, near the water's edge. By August the eggs have hatched into tadpoles by the hundreds of thousands and quickly evolve into giant wriggling masses of tiny toadlets ready to make the perilous journey back into the forest. Encounter this natural wonder August through September at Little Three Creek Lake—a short, just over a mile, walk from the trailhead (Hike #12)—and raise your awareness about an amphibian on Oregon Department of Fish and Wildlife's sensitive species list. Watch your step! Kids will love this outing; bring a bucket along with your picnic and help toadlets cross the trail into the woods. *alltrails.com*

Identify Cascade Peaks at the Dee Wright Observatory

The hand-hewn observatory rises from the black lava fields like a primitive battlement guarding an exceptional panoramic view of the Oregon Cascades. Located at the summit of McKenzie Pass, it was built from local lava in the 1930s by the CCC and is fully accessible. At the top, open window slits target and identify Cascade Peaks, including Mount Jefferson, all three of the Sisters, and Mount Hood. The upper level has a large standing brass compass to point out even more peaks. Try the Lava River Interpretive Trail; its signage describes the geology of the area and it's wheelchair accessible—but steep in places. *fs.usda.gov*

Explore a Volcano the Size of Rhode Island

The Newberry Volcano is the largest by size in the Cascade Range. The broad shield volcano spreads over 1,200 square miles and continues to be seismically and geothermally active. Begin with a visit to the Lava Lands Visitor Center, the interpretive hub of the Newberry National Volcanic Monument. Hike or bike the paved, fully accessible, 5.5-mile Sun-Lava Path, or take a shuttle to the top of Lava Butte, a cinder cone capped by a crater, with 360-degree views. *fs.usda.gov*

Spelunk the Lava River Cave

Bring two sources of light, warm clothing, and sturdy shoes to explore the inside of the earth on this remarkable hike at the Newberry National Volcanic Monument. The mile-long lava tube dives down to a combination of boardwalks, rocky surfaces, and stairways that wind through the ancient volcanic tunnel. The cave maintains a constant 40 degrees inside and creates two ecosystems at the entrance. One is dry and characterized by ponderosa pine and bitterbrush. The other, where condensation from the cool cave air meets the warm outer air, fosters plants like false Solomon's seal and wax currant, typically found in wetter climates. Listen to your eerie returning voice in Echo Hall and shine your light on the Sand Garden's delicate pinnacles—this is a hike like no other. Northwest Forest Pass required; no pets allowed; if you've visited other caves, change clothing to reduce spread of the bat disease white-nose syndrome. *fs.usda.gov*

THREE FINGERED JACK, OREGON

Season of Snow

The Bend/Sisters region is a high-use area in all seasons. Expect crowded conditions on weekends at all developed recreation sites, with parking at Sno-Parks filling up by midmorning. Most of the trails featured here start from one of the many Sno-Parks in the Bend/Sisters area. Trail maps are available at most Sno-Parks. Note that snowshoers must stay to the side on groomed trails. Check the weather forecast and road conditions before leaving home.

SNOWSHOE AND CROSS-COUNTRY SKI TRAILS

Guided USFS Snowshoe Tour

Begin this free ranger-guided snowshoe tour at the snowshoe hut in Mt. Bachelor's West Village. The informative trips are offered daily during school holiday breaks and then on weekends through March. For more information, call 541-383-4055. *mtbachelor.com*

Tumalo Mountain

Follow the tracks of previous trampers on this unmarked trail to the top of conical Tumalo Mountain. At the summit marvel over the breathtaking views of the Three Sisters and the high desert that spreads beneath you. Plan on 4 to 5 hours for this moderate trail, which begins at Dutchman Flat Sno-Park. *alltrails.com*

Wanoga Snow Play Area Sno-Park

This Sno-Park has it all—sledding, snowshoeing, fat biking, and cross-country skiing. There's an excellent flat trail for young children and beginner snowshoers that's only a mile long, as well as an easy 2-mile trail for cross-country skiers. It's dog friendly, with groomed trails for both cross-country skiers as well as snowshoers.

Swampy Lakes and Meissner Sno-Parks

There are 27 miles of ungroomed trail options at Swampy Lakes for all skill levels. Swampy Lakes also accesses the trails of Meissner Sno-Park, adding 25 more miles of exceptional terrain, most of them groomed. There are multiple dedicated snowshoe trails at both parks, as well as a wide range of options for both classic and skate skiers. Begin your day at Meissner with a stop at the Nordic lodge, where you'll find brochures with trail maps. Between the two Sno-Parks there are also five warming shelters with outstanding views, perfect for pulling out a thermos of hot chocolate and taking a break. Love the trails? Consider donating at the Meissner Nordic lodge's box to support grooming operations. On their website, the Central Oregon Nordic Club has all the information you'll need on snowshoe and cross-country ski trails in the area: conordicclub.org.

DOWNHILL SKI AND SNOWBOARD TRIPS

Mt. Bachelor vs. Hoodoo

Mt. Bachelor and Hoodoo are two very different options for downhill skiers and snowboarders. Bachelor is big and brawny, with 11 lifts (including 8 high-speed quads), and Hoodoo is laid-back with fewer crowds for its 5 chairs. Mt. Bachelor has 101 runs, 7 terrain parks from beginner to advanced, and multiple lodge options for fueling on the slopes. Hoodoo is steeper and cheaper: 40 percent of its 34 runs are black diamond, it offers deeply discounted lift tickets on Thrifty Thursdays, and it's the only place in the area to night ski.

SLEDDING AND TUBING

Wanoga Snow Play Area Sno-Park

Wanoga was specifically constructed for families and groups who wanted a snow slope dedicated to sledding and tubing. For the price of a Sno-Park permit you can play all day, rest in the warming shelter beside the woodstove, and even build a bonfire outdoors in one of the fire pits. Have a tube tailgate party and make a day of it.

Autobahn Tubing Park

At Hoodoo ski area, you have a choice of dedicated groomed tubing hills and can pick your speed. A rope tow will haul you up, or you can walk up the hill. There's a warming shack with snacks available, and tubes are included with the price of the ticket.

Mt. Bachelor's Snowblast Tubing Park

Ride the rope tow up the hill, then fly down one of the multiple lanes. Advance reservations are a good idea. Tubes are included with the price of the ticket.

EXPLORE MORE ADVENTURES

Trek to a Yurt in the Mountains

Head to the mountains and rent one of the Three Sisters Backcountry yurts beneath Tam McArthur Rim. A snowmobile shuttle takes you and your gear 6 miles to the yurt. Then spend the days cross-country skiing the spectacular and varied terrain and return to woodstove warmth and a wood-fired sauna. The yurts sleep 6 and have full kitchens. *threesistersbackcountry.com*

Go Birding with the Family

Sunriver Nature Center and Observatory offers a family outing to discover the overwintering birds in the area—including woodpeckers, hawks, owls, finches, and sparrows—on easy snow-packed trails. A wonderful introduction to the world of birds for little hikers. Bring your own binoculars or you can rent them from the center. *snco.org*

Learn to Ice Skate

Learn to forward swizzle, backward wiggle, and two-foot glide at Bend Parks and Recreation's ice rink, the Pavilion. During the winter season the rink opens to the public with plenty of activities, including private ice-skating lessons to help you master the giddy thrill of gliding on ice. The outdoor seating area has fire pits and heaters if you simply want to watch. *bendparksandrec.org*

CRATER LAKE, OREGON

Crater Lake, Oregon

Giiwas

Crater Lake is not a crater but a deep-water caldera created 7,700 years ago from the violent eruption and collapse of Mount Mazama—not one volcano, but a complex of overlapping shield and composite volcanoes. It's one of the deepest lakes in the world, at 1,932 feet, and it's filled with the pristine and translucent water from snowmelt and rain. No inlets or rivers with their sediment enter the lake, giving it an electric-blue color and making it one of the cleanest and clearest lakes in the world. The Klamath tribe's oral history named the deep caldera Giiwas, an "Abode for the Creator," and recounts their ancestors living through the eruption and collapse of Mount Mazama. The Klamath people regard Giiwas as a sacred site. Historically they journeyed here for dangerous undertakings that, if successfully completed, bestowed great spiritual powers, and they were resistant to point out Giiwas to early explorers. But in 1853 John Hillman and his group stumbled upon the exquisite lake he named Deep Blue Lake. The lake was captured on film in 1874, introducing its stunning beauty to the nation, including William Gladstone Steel, who pushed and lobbied relentlessly to make it a national park. In 1902 his dream became a reality.

Crater Lake is a popular national park, and there are few options for accommodations. Visit this extraordinary place in September when the crowds thin, the lodge and campgrounds have more availability, and the hiking is sublime, with cooler temperatures and fewer people on the trails. It's a high-elevation lake; the rim elevation alone averages between 7,000 and 8,000 feet. Give yourself at least 24 to 36 hours to acclimate before hiking or cycling, and drink water frequently! Your body loses a great deal of water not only from the dry air, but also from the increased respiration that higher elevations demand.

Begin your visit at one of the two park visitor centers: the Steel Visitor Center or the Rim Visitor Center. The staff can help with trip planning, the weather forecast, and questions you may have about the area. The Steel Visitor Center is open year-round except for December 25. The ranger station headquarters are located in the visitor center complex; here you can get the backcountry permit needed for all overnight excursions (no permit needed for day hikes). The permits are not issued more than one day in advance and must be obtained in person at headquarters

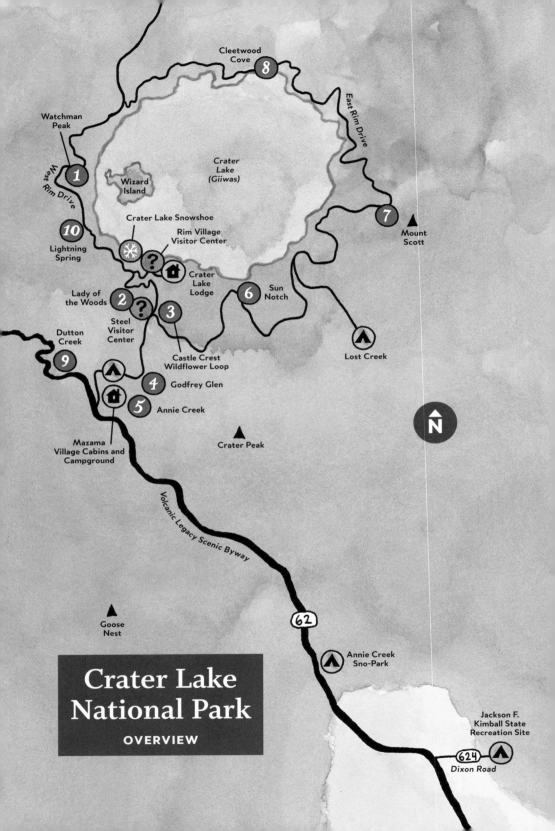

Cleetwood Cove
8

East Rim Drive

Watchman Peak

West Rim Drive

1

Wizard Island

Crater Lake (Giiwas)

7

Mount Scott

Crater Lake Snowshoe

10

Lightning Spring

Rim Village Visitor Center

❄

?

🏠

Crater Lake Lodge

Lady of the Woods

2

?

6

Sun Notch

Steel Visitor Center

3

Dutton Creek

9

🏕

Castle Crest Wildflower Loop

Lost Creek

🏕

4

Godfrey Glen

🏠

5

Annie Creek

Ⓝ

Mazama Village Cabins and Campground

Crater Peak

Volcanic Legacy Scenic Byway

Goose Nest

62

Annie Creek Sno-Park

🏕

Crater Lake National Park

OVERVIEW

Jackson F. Kimball State Recreation Site

624

🏕

Dixon Road

during business hours. The Rim Visitor Center is open from late May to late September (dates depending on when the snow starts) and is closed for the winter. Note there is no cell or internet service within Crater Lake National Park and very limited service at Crater Lake Lodge. As you will have paid your fee upon entrance or used your America the Beautiful Pass, there are no other passes needed for the hikes. *nps.gov*

Get Away

CAMPGROUNDS ▲

Mazama 🏃

Located in Mazama Village, which has a restaurant, gift shop, gas station, laundry facilities, and a camp store, this large campground has 214 sites, 75 percent of them reservable in advance and 25 percent first come, first served. The campground typically fills up by midafternoon. Pets allowed on leashes; closed in winter.

Lost Creek

This small campground of 16 walk-in tent-only sites is located on the road to Pinnacles Overlook. It's usually open in early July (depending on snow levels) and closes in mid-October. First come, first served; pets allowed on leashes.

Annie Creek Sno-Park

Ten miles south of the national park's Annie Spring entrance, this Sno-Park campground is open year-round. There are several primitive campsites along the creek, some with fire rings. It has vault toilets, picnic tables, and a log warming shelter with a woodstove and benches. Camping is free, but you must bring your own potable water. First come, first served; pets allowed on leashes.

Jackson F. Kimball State Recreation Site

This small 12-site campground is fabulous. The primitive but attractive sites are based at the headwaters of the Wood River. Not only is there fairly close access to Crater Lake National Park, but there's fishing and kayaking in the lagoon waterway of the river. There are vault toilets, but no potable water. First come, first served; pets allowed on leashes.

CABINS AND LODGES 🏠

Crater Lake Lodge ♿

Established in 1915, the lodge is a grande dame of history and hospitality. Listed on the National Register of Historic Places and overlooking the lake with majestic views, it is a wonderful place to relax after a day of exploring. There are 71 guest rooms and a restaurant with outdoor seating overlooking the lake. The lack of cell service and very limited internet available in the lobby are more than compensated for by spending glorious days outdoors. The lodge is open seasonally from late May to mid-October, and fills fast. Reservations highly recommended, particularly June through Labor Day in September.

The Cabins at Mazama Village ♿

The cabins aren't luxe, but they are only 7 miles from the lake and set in a tranquil ponderosa pine forest with several nearby hiking opportunities.

Season of Green

DAY HIKES

1. Watchman Peak 😊 ⚙️ 🌟

- Moderate
- 1.6 miles round trip out and back
- 420 feet elevation gain
- 1 hour

There's an expansive eagle's-eye view across the lake from the top of this short and relatively easy hike. The lookout at the top is used periodically as an active fire station. Avoid the crowds and arrive early in the morning; this is one of the most popular hikes in the park. *oregonhikers.org*

2. Lady of the Woods 😊 🚺 🐾

- Easy
- 0.7-mile loop
- 120 feet elevation gain
- 30 minutes

This hike is named for a fascinating unfinished sculpture of a woman embracing a large volcanic boulder. In 1917 a doctor named Earl Russell

Bush was staying in nearby housing helping to build the Rim Drive, and at the end of the season he stayed on for two extra weeks to carve, his first attempt at sculpting. He left the piece unfinished. Find a brochure guide to the loop at the trailhead behind the Steel Visitor Center. *craterlakeinstitute.com*

3. Castle Crest Wildflower Loop ☺ ⚲ ✿ �e

- Easy
- 0.4-mile loop
- 70 feet elevation gain
- 30 minutes–1 hour

A spectacular summer wildflower show is the draw on this short but diverse loop. The bowled meadow is flanked by Castle Crest Ridge and low moraines; several gushing springs generate lush conditions and produce a prolific display of wildflowers. Bring a wildflower guidebook with you and take advantage of the interpretive brochure available at the trailhead. *nps.gov*

4. Godfrey Glen ☺ ⚲ 🐾 ♿

- Easy
- 1.1-mile loop
- 50 feet elevation gain
- 45 minutes

An easy loop (accessible to all-terrain wheelchairs) with an eye-popping bonus at the end: a lush canyon punctuated with fluted spires of hardened ash, remnants of old vents from the Mazama volcanic explosion. Interpretive brochures at the trailhead add to your experience. *craterlakeinstitute.com*

5. Annie Creek ⚲ ✿ �e

- Moderate
- 1.8-mile loop
- 200 feet elevation gain
- 1–1.5 hours

The loop starts at the Mazama campground, meanders along the rim of Annie Creek Canyon, then switchbacks down to the crystal-clear waters of Annie Creek. Towering volcanic pinnacles greet you at the bottom, old vents from the eruption that have been cut by ancient streams. Make your way along the creek bottom and watch for water ouzels (American dippers), wildflowers, and several lovely picnic places. This is a hike that begs for attentive dawdling. Borrow the excellent interpretive guide at the trailhead for more natural history. *craterlakeinstitute.com*

6. Sun Notch ☺ 🏕 ✿ ☀️ ♿

- Easy
- 0.5 mile round trip
- 115 feet elevation gain
- 30 minutes

Don't let the mild statistics fool you; this trail offers fantastic views, particularly at sunset. You'll see the rocky Phantom Ship outcropping in the lake and great views of the Chaski slide and Dutton Cliff. All-terrain wheelchair accessible with help. *craterlakeinstitute.com*

7. Mount Scott ✿ ☀️

- Moderate to difficult
- 5 miles round trip out and back
- 1,250 feet elevation gain
- 3–4 hours

I heard a wolf howl in a southwest valley on the climb to Mount Scott. Rare, transcendent, it made me pause to listen and catch my breath. The trailhead lies at 7,688 feet and climbs to nearly 9,000 feet, the highest point in the park. From the top you have a panoramic view of the Eastern Cascades, several of the great volcanoes, and the Klamath Basin. The basin is part of the Pacific Flyway, a major route for migratory birds, and teems with bird life. Bring a coat; the summit is windy even in summer. *craterlakeinstitute.com*

8. Cleetwood Cove ☀️

- Difficult
- 2.2 miles round trip out and back
- 700 feet elevation gain
- 3 hours

Cleetwood Cove Trail is the only legal way to the shore of the lake, and it's a doozy coming back up the steep trail—equivalent to climbing 65 flights of stairs. The hike is not recommended for anyone with health or mobility issues. Fishing is allowed here, but the water is too cold for swimming other than a quick dip. *nps.gov*

MULTIDAY BACKPACKING

9. Dutton Creek ⚙ 🦌

- Backcountry permit
- Moderate to difficult
- 4.8 miles round trip out and back
- 1,050 feet elevation gain
- 4–6 hours

This hike descends steadily for over a thousand feet through hemlock woods and meadowed openings, then meets the Pacific Crest Trail at 2.4 miles. Here, you'll camp at Dutton Creek. For a longer loop trail, go north the next morning on the PCT for 4.2 miles, then turn east on the Lightning Spring Trail (Hike #10) and hike 4 miles back out to Rim Drive. *craterlakeinstitute.com*

10. Lightning Spring ☺ ⚙

- Backcountry permit
- Easy
- 1.7 miles round trip out and back
- 250 feet elevation gain
- 1 hour

The Lightning Spring campsite is located less than a mile from the trailhead. The springs are small, some just seeps, but the campsite is shaded by tall hemlocks. It's a gentle, family-friendly hike to the springs that continues moderately on for 3.4 miles to intersect with the Pacific Crest Trail—a good hike excursion the next morning. *craterlakeinstitute.com*

EXPLORE MORE ADVENTURES

Cycle the Rim

The most popular cycling trip in the park is the grueling but beautiful 33-mile Rim Drive, which circles Crater Lake with an elevation gain of 3,800 feet. Traditionally, for two Saturdays each September, the East Rim Drive is closed to vehicles and bicyclists can join the Ride the Rim event for 24 miles of traffic-free cycling. *ridetherimoregon.com*

Fish for Kokanee Salmon

There are no fish native to Crater Lake, but between 1888 and 1941 it was stocked with seven different species of fish, two of which thrive today: the kokanee salmon, which is a landlocked sockeye salmon, and rainbow trout. You can fish for both from the shore accessed by the Cleetwood Cove Trail (Hike #8) and from the docks and shore of Wizard Island via scheduled boat tours that leave from Cleetwood Cove. Fishing is also permitted in all creeks and streams in the park except for Lost Creek and Sun Creek, both closed to increase the population of native bull trout.

Catch the Sunrise

"Where's the best place to watch sunrise at Crater Lake?" I asked the ranger at the park entrance. Without hesitation he said, "Cloudcap Overlook. The sun is at your back, and the lake is still." He was right. Check the sunrise time and arrive 20 minutes earlier for the radiant dawn show.

Take a Boat Tour to Wizard Island

During the summer the company Crater Lake Hospitality offers eight daily boat tours and two shuttles for independent exploration on Wizard Island. Join a park ranger and learn more about this deep-water caldera as you circumnavigate the lake. Two of the offered tours stop at Wizard Island for three hours. *travelcraterlake.com*

Visit Fort Klamath and Upper Klamath Lake

Fort Klamath is 16 miles from the Annie Creek entrance to Crater Lake National Park and is listed on the National Register of Historic Places for its deep Oregon Trail history. The museum at Fort Klamath is worth a stop, but it's the Upper Klamath National Wildlife Refuge, covering 133 square miles, that bird-lovers and anglers won't want to miss. Upper Klamath Lake and adjacent wetlands form the Klamath Basin, one of the largest freshwater ecosystems west of the Great Lakes. In spring and fall, the waterways are a stopping point for over a million birds through the Pacific Flyway, a major migratory route. The more than 300 species include egrets, sandhill cranes, white-faced ibis, raptors, ducks, geese, and swans. You can rent a boat or a canoe to explore these waters, or many local concessionaires offer rentals and guided tours. Try the Upper Klamath Canoe Trail, a marked 9.5-mile water journey that weaves through the rich ecosystem of the Klamath Marsh. *paddling.com/paddle/trips/upper-klamath-canoe-trail-in-oregon*

Season of Snow

Crater Lake receives up to 44 feet of snow each winter. The park is open year-round, but the north entrance road and Rim Drive are closed to wheeled vehicles all winter. The west and south entrances are open to cars and plowed throughout the season. Keep in mind that traction tires or chains are required, check out the weather forecast, and be aware of alerts and road closures before leaving for the park.

SNOWSHOE TRAILS

Free-for-All Snowshoeing

Exploring the slopes and meadows of Crater Lake by snowshoe is a popular winter activity. The Rim Village gift shop offers snowshoe rentals, and the winter park newspaper will list their current cost and availability as well as suggested trails, all ungroomed, that range from easy to difficult. The Rim Drive is closed to vehicles in the winter months (generally November through May), and it becomes a trail for snowshoers and cross-country skiers. *nps.gov*

Guided Snowshoe

On a 2-hour off-trail snowshoe walk led by a park ranger, learn how plants and animals survive the harsh winters. The walks are offered on weekends from early December through April and every day from December 26 to January 5. The no-charge tour is 1 to 2 miles through moderate to difficult terrain along the lake's rim, through forests and meadows. Free snowshoe rentals; space is limited and advance reservations are required by calling the Steel Visitor Center at 541-594-3100. *nps.gov*

CROSS-COUNTRY SKI TRAILS

Free-for-All Cross-Country

Cross-country skiing is a wild and free experience at Crater Lake. There are many marked and unmarked routes, none are groomed, and they can be deep and difficult to follow, with skiers often breaking trail through unmarked snow. Maps and descriptions of the ski trails can be found in the winter edition of the park newspaper. There are no ski rentals within the park. *nps.gov*

SLEDDING

There are ample places for sledding within the park, but no designated sled hills or snow play areas—it's all an open playground. Choose a place free of trees; there are many meadows with perfectly pitched slopes. One of the most popular sledding hills is the open meadow next to Crater Lake Lodge at the Rim Village.

EXPLORE MORE ADVENTURES

Snow Trek around Crater Lake

Each year a handful of skiers and snowshoers choose to make their way around the lake in winter, an exceptional adventure, but one that requires winter camping experience and strong outdoor and navigation skills. In good conditions the 31-mile loop takes around 3 days to complete. With storms, which are common, it can take longer; plan wisely. A backcountry permit is required for the entire tour. *nps.gov*

Winter Camp

Test your winter skills and enjoy the distinct pleasure of snow camping in a gorgeous landscape. Here are a few ideas:

WEST RIM DRIVE CAMPOUT: This is an out-and-back trip with the distance up to you. Many choose to go out for 1 or 2 nights and camp between Discovery Point and North Junction. Be aware of the avalanche area around Watchman Peak.

EAST RIM DRIVE CAMPOUT: On this round trip out and back trip the most popular camping is between the summit of the drive's first climb and Sun Notch. Take care near Vidae Falls and the Sun Notch avalanche areas and use the avalanche bypass route.

ANNIE CREEK SNO-PARK: Located 10 miles south of the Annie Spring entrance, this Sno-Park campground is a good base for winter activities in the park. There are vault toilets, picnic tables, and a log warming shelter with a woodstove and benches. Camping is free, but you must bring your own potable water. First come, first served; pets allowed on leashes.

CRATER LAKE, OREGON

Acknowledgments

This book was researched and written through the pandemic and wildfires, park closures and social isolation, but I was never alone. My gratitude to Marti, my ready and willing companion when solo camping was burdensome; to my children and grandchildren for reminding me to look up when my eyes were locked on the trail. A huge thank-you to Nick Hall for his photographs, which make the book sing with visual arias, and to Jenna, my mapmaker and guide when I felt lost. Thank you to Tim McNulty, Doris and Gary, and Libby for warmly detailed answers to regional questions. Thank you to my Tias and Sorelle for walking side by side with me. I am grateful for the professional support of my agent, Rita Rosenkranz; Jonathan Tomhave, for shining a light on Indigenous peoples' integral role in our region; my fabulous illustrator, Chandler O'Leary, who nailed it with her maps and artwork; and my editor, Hannah Elnan, who offered the mountains to me. Most of all, my endless love and gratitude to PW, who patiently made room for all my returns with grace and humor.

HORSETAIL FALLS, OREGON

Bibliography

Barnes, Nathan, and Jeremy Barnes. *Alpine Lakes Wilderness: The Complete Hiking Guide*. Seattle: Mountaineers Books, 2019.

Blair Jr., Seabury. *Day Hike! Olympic Peninsula*. 4th ed. Seattle: Sasquatch Books, 2019.

Hill, Richard L. *Volcanoes of the Cascades: Their Rise and Their Risks*. Guilford, CT: Falcon, 2004.

Judd, Ron C. *Day Hike! Mount Rainier*. 4th ed. Seattle: Sasquatch Books, 2019.

McNulty, Tim. *Olympic National Park: A Natural History*. 4th ed. Seattle: University of Washington Press, 2018.

McQuaide, Mike. *Day Hike! North Cascades*. 4th ed. Seattle: Sasquatch Books, 2019.

Plumb, Gregory A. *Waterfall Lover's Guide Pacific Northwest*. 5th ed. Seattle: Mountaineers Books, 2013.

Romano, Craig, and Aaron Theisen. *Day Hiking Mount St. Helens*. Seattle: Mountaineers Books, 2015.

Sullivan, William L. *100 Hikes/Travel Guide Central Oregon Cascades*. 5th ed. Eugene, OR: Navillus Press, 2020.

Sullivan, William L. *100 Hikes/Travel Guide Northwest Oregon & Southwest Washington*. 5th ed. Eugene, OR: Navillus Press, 2020.

SOL DUC FALLS, WASHINGTON

Day Hike Index

HIKE	LENGTH	☺	🔥	⚙	🏃	🍃	🐾	★	♨	♿
Olympic Peninsula										
Big Meadow	0.25 mi			✔				✔		✔
Madison Creek Waterfalls	0.3 mi	✔	✔						✔	✔
Cirque Rim	0.5 mi			✔				✔		✔
High Ridge	0.5 mi			✔				✔		
Rain Shadow Loop	0.5 mi	✔	✔	✔				✔		
Sol Duc Falls	1.6 mi	✔	✔			✔		✔		
Marymere Falls	1.8 mi	✔	✔					✔		
Ranger Hole–Interrorem Nature Trail	2.1 mi	✔	✔				✔			
Staircase Rapids	2.2 mi	✔	✔							
Hurricane Hill	3 mi			✔				✔		
Quinault National Recreation Trails	4–10 mi	✔	✔			✔	✔			
Quinault River Pony Bridge	4.8 mi	✔	✔	✔		✔		✔		
Sunrise Ridge	5.2 mi	✔		✔			✔			
Upper Dungeness	6.8 mi	✔		✔		✔	✔			
Spruce Railroad Trail	8 mi	✔	✔							
Mount Baker										
Boyd Creek Interpretive Trail	0.5 mi	✔	✔	✔				✔		✔
Fire and Ice	0.5 mi	✔		✔				✔	✔	
Picture Lake	0.5 mi	✔		✔				✔	✔	✔
Shadow of the Sentinels	0.5 mi	✔	✔					✔		✔
Horseshoe Bend	2.4 mi	✔	✔	✔				✔		
Baker River	5 mi	✔	✔	✔			✔	✔	✔	
Excelsior Peak via Damfino Lakes	6.5 mi		✔	✔	✔			✔	✔	
Yellow Aster Butte	7.5 mi		✔	✔				✔	✔	
Skyline Divide	9 mi		✔	✔	✔			✔	✔	
Baker Lake	14 mi	✔	✔	✔			✔	✔	✔	

Mount Hood

HIKE	LENGTH	😊	🔥	⚘	🌿	🐦	🐾	★	♨	♿
Little Zigzag Falls	1 mi	✓	✓	✓			✓		✓	
Trillium Lake Loop	1.9 mi	✓	✓	✓		✓	✓			
Mountaineer Trail Loop	2.7 mi		✓	✓				✓		
Lost Lake Loop	3.2 mi	✓	✓	✓	✓	✓	✓			
Mirror Lake	4.4 mi	✓	✓	✓			✓	✓		
Zigzag Overlook	4.4 mi	✓	✓	✓			✓			
Cascade Streamwatch Loop	5 mi	✓				✓	✓	✓		✓
Old Salmon River	5 mi	✓	✓	✓		✓	✓			
Umbrella Falls/Sahale Falls Loop	5 mi	✓	✓	✓	✓		✓		✓	
Ramona Falls Loop	7.1 mi		✓	✓		✓		✓	✓	

Deschutes National Forest

HIKE	LENGTH	😊	🔥	⚘	🌿	🐦	🐾	★	♨	♿
Head of the Metolius	0.5 mi		✓			✓	✓	✓		✓
Fall River Loop	1.9 mi		✓			✓	✓		✓	
Smith Rock State Park Canyon	3.3 mi		✓			✓	✓			
Black Butte	4 mi						✓	✓		
Crooked River Trail	4.4 mi		✓	✓		✓	✓			
Canyon Creek Meadows	4.5 mi			✓		✓	✓	✓		
Twin Lakes Loop	4.5 mi		✓	✓		✓	✓			
West Metolius River	5.5 mi		✓	✓		✓			✓	
Chus Falls	5.7 mi			✓		✓	✓		✓	
Carl Lake	10 mi			✓	✓	✓	✓			

Crater Lake

HIKE	LENGTH	😊	🔥	⚘	🌿	🐦	🐾	★	♨	♿
Castle Crest Wildflower Loop	0.4 mi	✓	✓	✓		✓				
Sun Notch	0.5 mi	✓	✓	✓				✓		✓
Lady of the Woods	0.7 mi	✓	✓				✓			
Godfrey Glen	1.1 mi	✓	✓				✓			✓
Watchman Peak	1.6 mi	✓		✓				✓		
Annie Creek	1.8 mi		✓	✓		✓				
Cleetwood Cove	2.2 mi							✓		
Mount Scott	5 mi			✓				✓		

MOUNT ST. HELENS, WASHINGTON

Index

Ready for more PNW adventures?

Check out *By the Shore: Explore the Pacific Northwest Coast Like a Local*, also by Nancy Blakey.

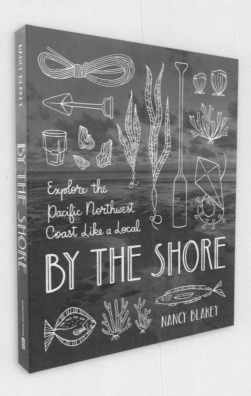

This guide to the iconic Pacific Northwest coast includes:

- Squid jigging
- Clam digging
- Crabbing
- Salmon derbies
- Homemade sea salt
- Bioluminescence
- Meteor showers
- Storm watching

- Bonfires
- Wish boats
- Driftwood forts
- Tide pools
- Whale watching
- Paddle trips, bike trips, and road trips

About the Author

Jenna Hall

NANCY BLAKEY is the author of *By the Shore: Explore the Pacific Northwest Like a Local*. She grew up in the Pacific Northwest and currently lives and writes on an island in Puget Sound. *The Mountains Are Calling* led her to fall in love with volcanoes and waterfalls. Visit her at NancyBlakey.com.